Praise for Culinary Arts Career Starter...

"*Culinary Arts Career Starter* is an excellent resource for any person researching a career as a culinarian. It is armed with useful, practical information which will help the prospective culinarian make his/her choice. The text is first-rate and I highly recommend this as a primer for anybody wishing to know how to get started on a culinary career. On behalf of the American Culinary Federation, I offer this text our whole-hearted support."

Noel C. Cullen, Ed.D., CMC, AAC, National ACF President, American Culinary Federation

"Author Mary Masi has created a thorough resource on the culinary arts field that is sure to help anyone who is thinking of entering the food service profession. Extensive appendices are an invaluable addition to an already strong and well-written guide."

L. Timothy Ryan, CMC, Executive Vice President, The Culinary Institute of America

CULINARY ARTS CAREER STARTER

by Mary Masi

LearningExpress ♦ New York

Copyright © 1999 LearningExpress, LLC.

All rights reserved under International and Pan-American Copyright Conventions.
Published in the United States by LearningExpress, LLC, New York.

Library of Congress Cataloging-in-Publication Data

Masi, Mary.
    Culinary arts career starter / Mary Masi.
        p.   cm.
        ISBN 1–57685–205–9
        1. Food service—Vocational guidance.   I. Title.
TK911.3.V62M363   1999
647.95'023—dc21   98–52533
                                        CIP

Printed in the United States of America
9 8 7 6 5 4
First Edition

Regarding the Information in this Book
Every effort has been made to ensure accuracy of directory information up until press time.
However, phone numbers and/or addresses are subject to change. Please contact the respective organization for the most recent information.

For Further Information
For information on LearningExpress, other LearningExpress products, or bulk sales, please write to us at:

    LearningExpress®
    900 Broadway
    Suite 604
    New York, NY 10003

Or visit us at:
    www.learnatest.com

CONTENTS

ABOUT THE AUTHOR

Mary Masi, M. A., is the founder of InfoSurge, a company specializing in writing, research, and editorial consulting. Previously, she worked in the editorial division of John Wiley & Sons, Inc., and before that, as a college English instructor.

ACKNOWLEDGMENTS

I would like to thank all of the culinary arts professionals who shared with me their insights into the profession and their resource materials. Specific thanks go to Executive Chef Timothy Rodgers, Team Leader for Curriculum and Instruction, Meat and Garde Manger, at the Culinary Institute of America; Heidi Cusick, Director of Education and Programs at the American Institute of Wine and Food; Chef Mike Nipper for the tour of the Clubhouse kitchens at the Westin Innisbrook resort; Chef Charles Ciufi, president of the Florida Suncoast Cooks and Chefs Association; Chef and Restaurateur Mary Cannataro of Malia's Cucina; Chef Geraldine Born, Culinary Educator at Pinellas Technical Education Center; Chef Sharon Odmann, Owner of Kiyote Cowboy Cookery & Personal Chef Services; Executive Chef Alex Darvishi at the Meridian Hills Country Club; Kim O'Donnel, Producer of Food and Restaurants for Washingtonpost.com; Author and Executive Chef Ann Cooper of the Putney Inn; Jennifer McAllister, Baking and Pastry Arts Student at Peter Kump's New York Cooking School; Julie Goings, Librarian in the Information Services department of the American Baking Institute; Phyllis Isaacson, Director of Information Services at the James Beard Foundation; Beverly Stuart, Assistant Director of Operations for the American Culinary Federation; and the following individuals at the National Restaurant Association: Kate McAloon, Information Specialist; Susan Kessler in Communications; and Jacqui Thomas in Member Services. Thanks also to James Gish, Christina Buffamonte, and Colleen Connors at LearningExpress. And special thanks goes to Thomas for cooking all those gourmet dinners.

Permission to reprint the list of salaries for food service professionals was granted by the National Restaurant Association.

Permission to reprint the list of apprenticeship programs and formal job titles of culinary arts professionals was granted by the American Culinary Federation.

INTRODUCTION

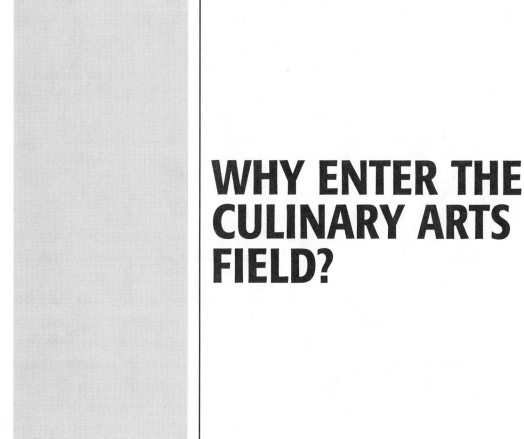

WHY ENTER THE CULINARY ARTS FIELD?

Do you want to have the opportunity to work with food, earn a good living, and meet lots of interesting people? If so, a career in the culinary arts may be just what you are looking for. Whether you are choosing your first career, or are simply considering a career change, this book is for you. It contains all the information you need to break into this exciting and growing field.

The possibilities seem endless when you start looking for career opportunities in the culinary arts field. You might choose to work for a four-star restaurant, become a personal chef, or start your own catering company. This rewarding field is expected to grow steadily through the year 2006, according to the Bureau of Labor Statistics. Many job openings for cooks and chefs will occur due to people transferring into other occupations or retiring. However, the growth of the industry and the changing demographic makeup of America will create a lot of new jobs as well. Here are several reasons for the growth of jobs in the culinary arts field:

- increase in the population of people over 55, who tend to eat out more
- increase in the number of people in the 16–24 age group, who typically work in the food service industry in large numbers
- increase in average household income, enabling people to eat out more
- a shift from a manufacturing-based economy to a service-based one
- more double-income households

All of these changes point to solid growth in the foodservice industry. Indeed, the career opportunities available in the culinary arts field today are many and varied. This book will show you what those opportunities are and how you can take advantage of them.

In chapter one, you'll get an inside look at the best jobs in culinary arts today—from sauté cook to pastry chef to executive chef and more. You'll find practical information such as job descriptions, typical income levels, trends in educational background, fast-growing geographic locations, types of employers, and personality traits and abilities needed for the hottest jobs in the culinary arts. Chefs from across the country give you the inside scoop on how to break into and succeed in this exciting field. Take the quiz included in this chapter to help you decide if a culinary arts career is right for you.

In chapter two, you'll find examples of courses that are taught in actual culinary arts training programs from different colleges, institutes, and universities across the country. These program descriptions will give you an idea of the different types of training programs available and how much time you would have to devote to each one. Tips on how to evaluate the various programs are included.

Chapter three contains a directory of culinary arts training programs, which is a representative listing of schools across the country, alphabetically by state. So if you're considering moving to a new city, you can check out that city's culinary schools too. All training programs include school name, address, phone number and, where available, the fax number and Internet address, so you can contact each school directly to get more information and application forms.

CHAPTER | 1

This chapter shows you what the hottest job opportunities are in the culinary arts field, from line cooks to pastry chefs and more. You'll find out the typical responsibilities and average salaries for each job, and you'll see which personal traits and abilities will help you succeed. There's an overview of different types of employers, and finally, a quiz to help you decide if a career in culinary arts is right for you.

THE HOTTEST CULINARY ARTS JOBS

So you're interested in working with food! A wealth of opportunities is available in the growing field of culinary arts. Many high school graduates, career-changers, and others are drawn into this multi-billion dollar industry every year. Indeed, the food service industry is the number one retail employer in the United States—it employs more than nine million people. Chefs, cooks, and other kitchen workers make up a large percentage of the food service industry, and the chances for landing a great job in this exciting field are excellent. In fact, the Bureau of Labor Statistics predicts that by the year 2005, the demand for trained chefs will exceed the supply. What does that mean? It means that trained culinary arts professionals will be able to command higher salaries, more benefits, and extra perks from their employers. This field has experienced overwhelming growth in the past decade—the number of job openings for skilled bread and pastry bakers and restaurant chefs and cooks has grown dramatically:

Job Title	Percentage of Growth from 1983 to 1996
Bread and pastry bakers	92%
Restaurant chefs and cooks	78%

Since continued job growth is expected, now is the time to get the necessary training, break into the field, and advance in your culinary career.

WHY ENTER THE CULINARY ARTS FIELD?

For many people, the decision to enter the culinary arts field stems directly from their love of food. Whether that love of food was created from a happy childhood filled with hours in a warm kitchen surrounded by different delicious smells, from a voracious appetite, or from a love of reading cookbooks, it's a passion that pulls many people into the field. Of course, other people have very practical reasons for entering the field. They want a job with a good future and good prospects for advancement. Perhaps they can't stand working from 9 to 5 in an office. Well, cooking or baking in a professional kitchen definitely offers an unusual work environment.

Read on to find out more about the benefits of having a career in the culinary arts. While not all jobs offer the same working conditions, here are several common reasons that people enter this exciting field.

Love of Working with Food

People who truly enjoy working with food are drawn to the culinary arts every day. Whether you are a high school student, a community college graduate, or a career-changer with years of experience in another field, the culinary arts offers you an exciting chance to work with food. If you like to experiment by cooking new dishes, finding new ingredients, and seeking out different spices, you may be a candidate for a culinary career. Many chefs say that their love of food as children was their draw into the field. Perhaps your grandmother let you help bake fresh bread, or you watched with fascination as your father cut and chopped a myriad

Desire to Open A Restaurant

Many students entering culinary arts schools today say their dream is to open their own restaurant. They hope to enjoy a certain level of autonomy and to be able to express their creativity and culinary skill in a restaurant of their own making. While the road to becoming a chef/restaurateur is long and arduous, the ones who make it enjoy a special status in the culinary world. See chapter six for more information about opening a restaurant.

Now that you've seen many of the benefits of working in the culinary arts, you need to perform a self-evaluation to see if you have the traits and abilities necessary to succeed in this demanding but satisfying career.

DO YOU HAVE WHAT IT TAKES?

Perhaps you are interested in getting into the culinary arts field, but you aren't sure what personality traits or personal abilities are needed. Well, wonder no more! You need the ability to work as part of a team, discipline, personal cleanliness, organization skills, and a keen sense of taste and smell. Chef Timothy Rodgers, a Team Leader for Curriculum and Instruction in Meat and Garde Manger at the Culinary Institute of America, says, "To succeed and make it to the top in this industry, you need to have several abilities in addition to culinary skills: dexterity, passion, perseverance, patience, and adaptability." Read on to find out what else it takes to make it in the culinary field today.

Physical Stamina

Physical stamina and endurance are the key to success in a professional kitchen. Mary Cannataro, a chef in Chicago, Illinois, tells prospective culinarians, "Working in this field is tougher than most people think it is. It requires a lot of hard work and a great deal of physical stamina." Standing on your feet for long periods of time and lifting heavy pots, bags of supplies, and other heavy kitchen equipment can take its toll. While you may not have considered this point before, the importance of physical stamina cannot be overlooked in your personal assessment. Perhaps you'll need to begin an exercise regime in your spare time to increase your level of physical endurance. Indeed, Chef Cannataro emphasizes:

> When I was working from eight to 12 hours a day, I started making time to go to the health club to get into better physical shape to

handle the long days. It takes a lot out of you, so no matter how busy you are, you still have to take some time out for yourself.

You should be able to withstand the pressure and strain of working in close quarters at a very fast pace, standing for many hours at a time, lifting heavy kettles, and using hot ovens and grills. While injuries are seldom serious, some of the hazards of a culinary career include slips and falls, cuts, blisters, and burns.

Humility

While you may not consider many chefs to be humble, they probably had to start out that way. Since you'll probably be performing all sorts of mundane tasks at the beginning of your culinary career, it's best not to take a haughty attitude or say that any chore is beneath you. The ego of the chef in charge will take up the whole kitchen, so there won't be any room left for yours!

Good Communication Skills

Strong communication skills are needed to succeed in the culinary field because you will be working as part of a team in the kitchen. Additionally, an ability to communicate with your supervisors and peers will set you apart from the crowd and help you move ahead in your career. And if you decide to branch out and become a restaurateur, educator, or public speaker on a cooking show, you'll need well-honed communication skills.

Basic Math Skills

You may be surprised to find out how big a role mathematics plays in a culinary career. Jennifer McAllister, a student in the Pastry and Baking program at Peter Kump's New York Cooking School, offers this advice to prospective professional bakers:

> Develop your math skills—they are an important part of baking. You need to know how to convert recipes. For example, can you take a recipe for 20 scones and turn it into a recipe for seven dozen? Or take a recipe that calls for a round pan and convert it to fit a sheet pan? These are things you'll need to know. Practice using your math skills until they become second nature.

While math is especially important in the pastry and baking areas of specialization, basic math skills are used by all culinary professionals, including cooks and chefs. For example, you may need to halve a recipe to make a smaller portion of a particular dish or you may need to expand the recipe to serve 60 people instead of ten. Or, perhaps you'll need to convert a recipe from another country that is written in the metric system of measurement.

Attention to Detail

Taking care of details becomes very important during service, which is the busy rush time in restaurants. Will you be able to sauté five different entrees, create a special garnish, and remember to add the correct amount of salt to a dish all at the same time? Juggling several detail-oriented tasks at once is a skill that successful chefs have learned.

Management Skills

If you want to become a sous chef, chef, executive chef, or restaurateur, you'll need to work on your management skills. You'll want to know how to motivate and inspire the cooks on the hot line, the assistants in the pastry shop, and the servers on the floor. Luckily, there are many ways to obtain these skills. One of the most common is to take courses in restaurant management or business management from a local college or university. Another option is to take continuing education or correspondence courses sponsored by a culinary professional association.

CULINARY ARTS QUIZ

You must be interested in the culinary arts field—or you wouldn't be reading this book—but are you sure that you'd be suited for it? Here's a quick quiz to help you decide. Jot down your answers to the following questions and then take a look at the paragraph following the test.

_____ 1. Do you pay close attention to details?
_____ 2. Do you hate shopping for groceries?
_____ 3. Do you appreciate having variety in your work day?
_____ 4. Do you prefer working alone to working with other people?
_____ 5. Are you good at basic math?
_____ 6. Do you have trouble working quickly in demanding atmospheres?
_____ 7. Do you have strong physical stamina?

of ingredients before dumping them all into a pot of bubbling soup. The food memories and experiences of successful chefs are many and varied, but a common thread found in many chefs' backgrounds is their respect and appreciation for food.

Exciting Work Locations and Travel Opportunities

If you enjoy learning about new cultures and traveling extensively, a career in the culinary arts can help you do both. People everywhere need to eat, so just think about the wealth of opportunities in other countries to meet new people and experience new cultures. Many chefs recommend that you travel to another country to experience its food firsthand. Working for a year in Europe, Mexico, or the Middle East can help you to understand and learn about another culture's foods and customs. You can also find exciting work locations right here in America. Perhaps you want to ski in Aspen, Colorado. Well, there are several restaurants located there to serve the tourists and skiers who visit each year. You can apply to work in any number of kitchens and spend your free time on the slopes. Or if you love the beach, you can apply for a job at your favorite beach resort. The simple abundance of eating establishments throughout the country, and the world, offer a wealth of opportunities to an enterprising and adventurous person.

Chance to Work in a Glamorous Industry

The field of culinary arts has come a long way. It is no longer considered a trade, but a profession—in the past several years, the role of the chef has been greatly elevated. In fact, many chefs are now becoming celebrities in their own right. Chefs appear on television cooking shows and generate quite a devoted following of fans and supporters. In fact, an entire television network is now devoted to cooking and showcases the work of a great number of chefs every week. Check your local television listings for more information about the Television Food Network.

Many chefs own or work in high-quality upscale restaurants and are written about at great length in prestigious newspapers and magazines. Other chefs enjoy fame by working for Hollywood celebrities and writing cookbooks describing the recipes they create for their particular star. Many chefs command a six-figure income based on their fame, sterling reputation, or power to draw customers into a particular restaurant. Of course, the glamorous jobs are few and far between, but somebody has to get them and it might as well be you.

_____ 8. Do you want a routine that is the same every day?

_____ 9. Do you have good communication skills?

_____ 10. Do you value a high level of privacy and quiet time when you are at work?

_____ 11. Do you enjoy cooking meals for family or friends?

_____ 12. Do you feel that weekends must be spent with your friends or family?

_____ 13. Do your friends ask you to cook for them?

_____ 14. Do you grow faint and listless when in an excessively hot environment?

_____ 15. Have you ever asked someone for a copy of the recipe for a particular dish you enjoyed?

_____ 16. Do you get extremely nervous when working under tight, stressful deadlines?

_____ 17. Do you often eat out in fancy restaurants?

_____ 18. Do you have a hard time motivating yourself to do things?

_____ 19. Do you watch one or more cooking shows per week on television?

If you answered _yes_ to the majority of odd-numbered questions, and _no_ to the majority of even-numbered questions, then you'll probably want to go full steam ahead towards a culinary arts career. However, if you answered _yes_ to the majority of even-numbered questions, and _no_ to the majority of odd-numbered questions, then you may want to consider a job in a field related to the culinary arts but not necessarily in the high-stress world of a professional kitchen. (See chapter six to find out what these jobs are.)

JOB OPPORTUNITIES IN THE CULINARY ARTS FIELD

So you passed the quiz and now want to learn more about what types of jobs are available in the culinary arts field. As you'll see, many people are needed to produce the delicious meal you find placed before you when dining in a restaurant, from the executive chef to the prep cook to the grill cook to the sous chef to the pantry worker and more—the list of jobs goes on and on.

To differentiate workers in a restaurant, those who work in the kitchen are known as back-of-the-house staff. The people who serve customers, such as servers, bartenders, bussers, maitre d's, and hostesses, are called front-of-the-house staff.

Chef Positions

Landing one of the top back-of-the-house positions in an upscale restaurant often requires several years of experience in addition to formal culinary training. The highest position you can advance to in a culinary career is Master Chef.

Master Chef

The title of Master Chef or Master Pastry Chef is reserved for chefs who have achieved an impressive place in their career based on significant education, professional experience, and skill. The American Culinary Federation imparts the title of Master Chef only after extremely rigorous conditions are met. Applicants must pass a very difficult written and practical exam that is administered by other chefs and must possess significant skills in cooking, baking, food presentation, garde manger, nutrition, charcuterie, and food service management.

Executive Chef

Executive chefs hold a higher position in a kitchen than a chef or head chef. Executive chefs may even be responsible for a chain of restaurant kitchens in one region. To become an executive chef, you must have significant experience in the industry and a solid track record of success. The duties of an executive chef often include managing the kitchen staff, preparing work schedules, deciding which ingredients and supplies to order, computing costs, pricing and designing menus, creating dinner specials, hiring and firing staff, finding ways to increase productivity and decrease waste, and ensuring the quality of the food that the restaurant serves.

Chef

Chefs are recognized as skilled artists and creative craftspeople. It normally takes many long hours and years of experience to become a chef. In establishments that do not have an executive chef, the head chef (sometimes called the *chef de cuisine*) is responsible for managing all aspects of the kitchen. Therefore, chefs often perform many of the duties that an executive chef would perform, even though their title is *chef*. They are often responsible for hiring, firing, and managing the kitchen workers, as well as managing all the kitchen's equipment and supplies. Chefs may create menus and daily specials, cook the most important dishes, and use the most expensive ingredients in the kitchen. Occasionally, chefs are also the owner or part-owner of the restaurant in which they work.

Pastry Chef

Pastry chefs may specialize in breads, desserts, or other types of baked goods, and they often work in their own kitchen or in a separate part of the kitchen from the hot line and the garde manger or pantry station. Indeed, pastry chefs often have little interaction with other kitchen workers. Pastry chefs are responsible for baking breads and many of the desserts served at restaurants and other eating establishments. While the pace may not seem as hectic for a pastry chef as for a cook on the hot line, the duties are often intense and the hours long. A pastry chef often needs to rise very early in the morning to begin baking all the items that will be served at lunch. In addition to working in restaurants, pastry chefs work in retail bakeries, industrial baking plants, and institutions.

Pastry chefs have to know the math and chemistry needed for reducing, expanding, and experimenting with various recipes for baked goods. Pastry chefs in restaurants or small bakeries normally bake breads, rolls, pastries, pies, and cakes each day, doing most of the work by hand. They measure and mix ingredients, shape and bake the dough, and apply fillings and decorations. On the other hand, industrial bakers rely on sophisticated equipment to bake large quantities of breads and other baked goods. Some pastry chefs specialize in wedding cakes or desserts for banquets. The popularity of fresh baked breads and pastries should ensure continued rapid growth in the employment of bakers, according to the Bureau of Labor Statistics.

Sous Chef

A sous chef is normally responsible for assisting the head chef or executive chef in running the kitchen. Therefore, sous chef is often considered an administrative as well as a cooking position. In French, *sous* means *under*, so the sous chef is just under the head chef. Sous (pronounced SU) chefs are normally in charge of managing the kitchen when the head chef is not present. Depending on the size and type of the restaurant, there may be more than one sous chef—for example, a night sous chef and a day sous chef. In addition to cooking foods on the hot line, they often are responsible for a variety of other duties, such as training new hires, inspecting the work of the cooks, ordering supplies, and picking up slack during rush times if emergencies occur at any particular station. They are often responsible for overseeing and tasting certain foods before the foods are served to patrons. This job is often seen as the last step before becoming a full chef.

> ### Culinary Scoop
>
> **What is charcuterie?** *Charcuterie* is cooking or working with pork and other meat items, such as sausages, hams, pâtés, and terrines.

Hot Line Positions

In many professional kitchens, the kitchen staff are referred to as a *brigade*, a French term for a team of kitchen workers. You'll soon find out that many terms in the culinary world have been borrowed from the French language. While some of these terms may be unfamiliar, you'll get accustomed to them fairly quickly. Since every professional kitchen is different, the number of people making up the brigade in each kitchen will vary. A small kitchen may only employ a head chef and an assistant cook, while a large kitchen may include 20 or more *chefs de partie*, or cooks who prepare hot food—entrees, soups, pasta, vegetables and so on. Cooking these foods is called working on the *hot line*, and the various people who work on the hot line are referred to as *line cooks*. For example, the sauté cook, the grill cook, and the pasta cook are also known as line cooks. Each line cook has a station, and each station is referred to by the cook's title—so a sauté cook works at the sauté station, the grill cook works at the grill station, and so on. Here are some of the most common positions on the hot line.

Sauté Cook

The sauté cook is often the lead cook on the *hot line*. Guess what the sauté cook is responsible for? Why, sautéing food, of course. Sauté means to cook quickly in a small amount of oil over high heat. Sauté cooks must have experience in cooking a wide variety of meats, fish, and other foods, and if there isn't a separate sauce cook, they also make sauces to go with each entree. They often cook several different entrees at once, so their timing must be impeccable. The ability to prioritize tasks and maintain an organized flow of events around a hot stove for prolonged periods of time is necessary for sauté cooks. A sauté cook must be experienced enough not to overcook or undercook food and to prepare sauces for each type of meat, fish, poultry, or other food that they sauté. In most kitchens, the sauté cook is the highest position a cook on the hot line can attain.

Sauce Cook or Saucier

In very large upscale restaurants, you might find a position as a sauce cook, sometimes known as a saucier. These cooks are responsible for creating the sauces for all the dishes served on the menu. Nowadays, you won't find a sauce cook in many restaurants because in most cases, sauces are created by the head chef, the sous chef, or by one of the other hot line cooks.

Grill Cook

As you might imagine, a grill cook is a cook who uses a grill for cooking a variety of foods. Grill cooks may also employ the use of a broiler and an oven either separately or in conjunction with the grill. The job of a grill cook is similar to that of a sauté cook in that the ability to know when foods are cooked to perfection, not overcooked or undercooked, is paramount. In many cases, grill cooks prepare vegetables and other side dishes along with meat and fish entrees. As Americans move more towards healthy eating, the position of the grill cook increases in importance. In fact, some restaurants now feature the grill cook by placing him or her in full view of the public, either behind glass or a short wall. Many people enjoy the sights and sounds of a grill cook's work.

Fry Cook

Restaurants that serve ample amounts of fried foods usually employ a fry cook. Fry cooks are responsible for cooking all the fried foods in the restaurant, including appetizers such as fried onion rings and fried mozzarella sticks and main courses such as fried chicken or fried eggplant. In restaurants that do not offer a large variety of fried foods, the sauté or grill cook may take on the role of fry cook along with her or his other responsibilities.

Fish Cook

In some restaurants, usually those found along a water's edge, a fish cook joins the hot line to prepare and cook a wide variety of fish dishes. Where the demand is large enough to warrant a separate cook for fish, the fish cook enjoys a special status and is usually very experienced in a wide variety of fish dishes. Whether or not fish cooks do the actual de-boning and cutting of the fish depends on whether or not there is a separate butcher. If there isn't a separate butcher, the fish cook may need to cut, scale, and dress fish by removing the head, scales, and other inedible portions and cutting the fish into steaks or boneless fillets. Many fish cooks have experience as sauté or grill cooks, since the workload often overlaps, depending on the size and type of eating establishment.

Vegetable Cook

In restaurants or other establishments that are large enough to warrant it, vegetable cooks are added to the hot line to cook vegetables. Often, they work alongside the sauté and grill cooks and must employ teamwork skills so their vegetables are ready at the same time as the meat or fish entree. They may also coordinate or prepare various side dishes that are not vegetables along with their other responsibilities.

Pasta Cook

Cooks who serve up pasta from their own kitchen station have a demanding job. They may be responsible for creating fresh and innovative sauces and accompaniments in addition to pasta for entrees, appetizers, and side dishes. They need to know how long to prepare and cook each different type of pasta for many different dishes. Creating a wide variety of pasta from scratch is often a trademark of fine specialty and Italian restaurants.

Swing Cook

A swing cook helps out at whichever station needs it during the course of the shift. This position has many different names—roundsman, relief cook, tournant, floater, or kitchen helper. In some restaurants, there's more than one person who serves as a swing cook, during especially busy times.

Cold Kitchen Positions

The people who work with cold food are just as important to the overall success of the kitchen as those who work on the hot line. Here's an overview of a few of the cold kitchen positions.

Garde Manger

You may be wondering what *garde manger* means, although once you begin reading culinary arts literature, you'll come across the term often enough. Garde manger may mean slightly different things to different people, but it is a French term for *pantry* and its classic meaning is *cold foods.* You pronounce it GARD MAWN JAY. Nowadays, those who work in garde manger often create hot and cold appetizers, salads, sandwiches, desserts, and table decorations, such as ice sculptures. Additionally, a chef garde manger may be responsible for creating specialty salads, marinating foods, carving fruits and vegetables, and arranging food on the plate for presentation to the customer. In many kitchens, a chef garde manger is responsible for preparing foods for banquets and receptions. However, many restaurant kitchen staffs do not include a chef garde manger because their menu does not warrant it—a chef garde manger is more often found in hotels, banquet halls, or upscale, fine-dining restaurants. Here are a few traditional items that may be prepared by a chef garde manger, in addition to ice and tallow sculptures:

> **aspic:** a jelly of meat or tomato or other juice molded with meat or seafood and eaten as a relish
>
> **canapé:** a small piece of bread, toast, or a cracker spread with spiced meat, fish, cheese, or other item
>
> **galantine:** a mold of boned, seasoned, boiled white meat, such as chicken or veal, chilled and served in its own jelly
>
> **pâté de foie gras:** paste made from the livers of fattened geese

Pantry Cook

The pantry station is considered a subsection of garde manger because the pantry cook also works with cold foods. Depending on the hierarchy of a professional kitchen, a pantry cook may work under the supervision of a chef garde manger. Or, he may be the only person working the cold line and report directly to the head chef in the kitchen. Most pantry cooks spend their time preparing and plating cold foods, such as salads, salad dressings, appetizers, and desserts.

Butcher or Meat Cutter

In many restaurants, meat cutting is considered a part of garde manger. Meat cutting is a growing area of specialization within the culinary arts field. Meat cutters cut, trim, and prepare a wide variety of meats for use by the various cooks or chefs in their restaurant. Additionally, they may cut meat into steaks and chops, shape and tie roasts, and grind beef for use as chopped meat. Boneless cuts are prepared using knives, slicers, or power cutters, while bandsaws are required to carve bone-in pieces. Meat cutters often work with beef, poultry, pork, veal, lamb, fish, and wild game. They must cut each piece of meat into the correct size for each portion served in the restaurant, trim off the excess fat, and handle the skin. They may also prepare sausage and cure meat.

Meat cutters need manual dexterity, good depth perception, color discrimination, and good hand-eye coordination. Additionally, they need to have the strength to lift and move heavy and cumbersome pieces of meat.

Highly skilled meat cutters can save a great deal of money for their establishment by cutting and trimming the meat in the most cost-effective manner and by using as much of each type of meat as possible, thereby reducing waste. Some experienced meat cutters may also be responsible for buying meat, controlling inventory, and keeping records. Meat cutters often must undergo specific training in food safety and sanitation, due to the possible health hazards of mishandling meat. Meat cutting is also called meat fabrication in several professional kitchens, and most chefs have experience in many different types of meat cutting.

Entry-Level Jobs

The following two entry-level jobs offer a way to break into the culinary arts field, gain experience, and move ahead to more exciting positions. Don't discount the value of any position; instead, see it as a stepping stone to the job of your dreams.

Prep Cook or Kitchen Assistant

Prep cooks work under the direction of an experienced cook or chef, and they prepare food by cutting, measuring, cleaning, peeling, or grinding it. For example, they may spend an hour or two washing, peeling, and cutting up potatoes, then move on to measure out several different spices, and then spend several hours cleaning and cutting up vegetables for various dishes. They also may stir and strain soups and sauces. Each laborious task they take on saves the experienced cook time and effort, so this job is important to the success of the food establishment. If you've ever seen a cooking show on television, most likely a prep cook measured and chopped up all those nice little dishes of ingredients that the celebrity chef uses to make the recipe.

In many eating establishments, you can land a position as a prep cook or kitchen assistant without any previous experience. However, in highly selective upscale restaurants, you'll probably need some experience working or studying in a similar establishment or culinary school before you can break in. The type and size of the restaurant or institution makes a big difference in the qualifications needed to land a job. In a majority of restaurants, the job of prep cook is considered an entry-level position. Since many kitchen assistants do not have prior work experience, they normally start out earning minimum wage.

Pastry Assistant or Baker's Assistant

If baking and working with breads, desserts, and pastries sounds appealing, starting out as a pastry or baker's assistant may be the job for you. As a pastry assistant, you'll learn to measure, mix, and bake ingredients properly under the supervision of a pastry chef or baker. You may assist the pastry chef by preparing dough, either by hand or by using a machine, measuring ingredients, and performing other tasks. Your specific duties will depend on the size and type of establishment in which you find work. For example, if you become a pastry assistant at a four-star restaurant, you may help create the specialty desserts and breads that are served, normally at lunch and dinner.

If you work in a retail bakery that is located in the heart of a commercial district, you'll probably spend much of your time helping to bake bagels, muffins, croissants, and other breakfast items in the early morning hours. An important point to remember is that people who work in bakeries often have to start their workday in the wee hours. Someone has to be in the kitchen early, so the baked goods can be fresh and piping hot for the 6:00–9:00 morning rush hour.

Other Kitchen Positions

Fast-food restaurants, casual eateries, diners, and restaurants that are open for breakfast often have kitchen workers who do not make up a brigade, but who perform specific tasks that are needed for each type of establishment.

Specialty Fast-Food Cook

Specialty fast-food cooks prepare a limited selection of menu items in fast-food restaurants. They cook and package batches of food, such as hamburgers and fried chicken, pizza, and tacos, which are prepared to order or kept warm until sold. They often operate large-volume single-purpose cooking equipment. Employment of specialty fast-food cooks is expected to increase in response to the growth of the 16-24 age group, and the continuing fast-paced lifestyle of many Americans, according to the Bureau of Labor Statistics.

Short-Order Cook

Short-order cooks prepare foods in casual restaurants, diners, and coffee shops that emphasize fast service. They grill and garnish hamburgers, prepare sandwiches, fry eggs, and cook french fries, often working on several orders at the same time. Before the busy periods, short-order cooks slice meats and cheeses and prepare coleslaw or potato salad. During slow periods, they may clean the grill, food preparation surfaces, counters, and floors.

Breakfast Cook

Obviously not all establishments employ breakfast cooks since many are open only for lunch and dinner. However, the breakfast cook is an important person in many different types of restaurants and institutions. In addition to cooking common breakfast items such as eggs, bacon, and pancakes, many breakfast cooks create beautiful breakfast buffets and other specialty brunches. It is especially important for breakfast cooks to work quickly and efficiently since many people eating breakfast are in a hurry and do not intend to enjoy a leisurely meal—especially if they are rushing off to an important business meeting. Breakfast cooks have a range of foods to prepare depending on the menu of their establishment, but they often know how to cook eggs in at least 20–30 different ways (some celebrated chefs can cook eggs over 100 different ways!), several varieties of sausages, potatoes, Belgian waffles, blintzes, crepes, hot cereals, and other breakfast fare.

SALARIES, BENEFITS, AND UNIONS

Salaries and benefits you can expect as a culinary professional vary greatly depending on the type and size of the establishment in which you work. Some restaurants provide employees with free uniforms and free meals, but federal law permits employers to deduct from their employees' wages the cost or fair value of any meals or lodging provided, and some employers do so. Chefs, cooks, and other kitchen workers who work full time may receive benefits such as vacation days, sick days, and health insurance, but part-time workers generally do not. Benefits such as health insurance and retirement savings plans are most often found in large, well-established hotels, institutions, or franchise restaurants. Many small independent restaurants can't afford to offer such benefits to their workers, although a few do.

In some large hotels and restaurants, kitchen workers belong to unions. The principal unions are the Hotel Employees and Restaurant Employees International Union, the Service Employees International Union, and the United Food and Commercial Workers International Union. (See Appendix A for their contact information.)

Here are sample wages of kitchen workers as of 1995, according to a National Restaurant Association survey cited by the Bureau of Labor Statistics:

Job Title	Median hourly earnings	Hourly earnings for most people in this position
Cooks	less than $7.00	$6.00–$8.00
Short-order cooks	$6.50	$5.50–$7.25
Assistant cooks	$6.25	$5.50–$7.00
Salad preparation workers	$5.50	$5.25–$6.50
Bread and pastry workers	$6.50	$6.00–$7.75

Keep in mind, however, that experienced line cooks who work in upscale restaurants can make significantly more than the average wages listed above; for example, some highly skilled sauté cooks earn $15.00 or more an hour, bringing their annual salary to $30,000 or higher. Also, while the above figures are the most recent salary statistics available from the National Restaurant Association, they were derived in 1995, so you can safely assume the pay is somewhat higher today.

According to the American Institute of Baking, experienced industrial bakers with advanced certificates may currently earn approximately $30,000 a year, with restaurant and retail bakers and pastry chefs earning somewhat less, unless they have specialized training from one of the well-known culinary institutes. Some managers or owners of upscale bakeries in large cities may earn up to $100,000 a year or more.

Take a look at the following chart to get an idea of the average salaries for other food service professionals. The data from the chart is adapted and reprinted from a survey conducted by the National Restaurant Association in 1995. It shows the median salary and bonus income of all the respondents to the survey. For information on how to obtain a full version of this report, or to get an updated list of average salaries when it becomes available, contact the National Restaurant Association at 202-331-5900. (See Appendix A for their full mailing address and fax number.)

1995 Average Salaries for Selected Food Service Positions

	Base Salary		Annual Bonus	
	Total Number of Positions	Median Salary	Total Number of Positions	Median Bonus
Food and Beverage Director	265	$42,000	132	$4,000
Executive Chef	462	$38,000	212	$3,000
Chef	1,012	$30,000	317	$1,283
Sous Chef	980	$25,000	260	$1,000
Pastry Chef	215	$25,000	52	$570
Nutrition/Dietitian	47	$31,000	18	$350
Wine Steward	19	$26,000	5	N/A
Banquet Manager	192	$26,000	63	$2,225
Catering Manager	249	$28,000	61	$2,000
Unit Manager	6,457	$30,000	4,330	$3,000
Assistant Unit Manager	8,877	$23,000	4,607	$1,200
Night Manager	1,060	$20,800	137	$1,000
Manager Trainee	1,076	$20,800	139	$900
Dining Room Manager	557	$24,000	203	$1,025
Kitchen Manager	938	$24,000	459	$2,000

Reprinted and adapted, by permission, from *Compensation for Salaried Personnel in Food Service—1995*, page two. Copyright 1996 by the National Restaurant Association and Hay Group, Inc.

Some jobs include special benefits that are dependent on their location. For example, here is a job posting in Colorado that lists a ski pass as one of its benefits.

WANTED: Line Cooks

DESCRIPTION: An Aspen, Colorado Skiing Company Resort Hotel is looking for experienced cooks for our fine dining restaurant and banquet facilities. We offer a full four-mountain ski pass, 401K, health insurance, and temporary housing for eligible applicants.

MINIMUM REQUIREMENTS: 3–5 years' cooking experience and a desire to learn

SALARY INFORMATION: $9.00 to $13.00 per hour depending on experience

Many benefits exist for cooks and other culinary professionals, and if you don't mind relocating, you can find some unique and adventurous places to utilize your culinary skills. See chapter five for information about how to land a great culinary job.

Culinary Scoop

What is a toque? A *toque* is a tall, pleated, white hat that chefs wear. It is sometimes called a *toque blanche*, which is French for *white hat*. Some chefs claim that the 100 pleats in the tall hat stand for the 100 ways they can cook eggs!

TYPES OF EMPLOYERS

You can choose to work for a variety of employers in the culinary arts field, ranging from small casual restaurants to four-star fancy restaurants to institutions such as schools, hospitals, and more. According to the Bureau of Labor Statistics, about three-fifths of all chefs, cooks, and other kitchen workers were employed in restaurants and other retail eating and drinking places in 1996. One-fifth worked in institutions such as schools, universities, hospitals, and nursing homes. The remainder were employed by grocery stores, hotels, and many other organizations. In total, more than 3.4 million people held jobs in the food service field in 1996. See the following chart.

Job Title	Number of Jobs Held
Restaurant cooks	727,00
Institutional cooks	435,000
Bread and pastry bakers	182,000
Short-order and fast-food cooks	804,000
Other kitchen workers	1,252,000
Total:	3,400,000

Fine-Dining Restaurants

Upscale restaurants that offer their customers a fine-dining experience are considered among the best places to work by many chefs and cooks. These restaurants tend to offer many unusual and sometimes exotic foods on their menu and provide exquisite service in a tastefully decorated dining room. Fine-dining restaurants usually have high quality white tablecloths, instead of placemats or a bare table. They employ experienced chefs and cooks who prepare the food from scratch. Their menu items are more expensive than casual restaurants because they are made using premium, high-cost ingredients. Kitchen staffs often include one or more chefs, several line cooks, a bread and pastry baker, and prep cooks or assistant cooks. Each chef or cook usually has a special assignment, as discussed previously—sauté, grill, vegetables, pasta, fry, or sauce cook, for example. Executive chefs, chefs, and sous chefs coordinate the work of the kitchen staff and often direct the preparation of certain foods. They decide the size of servings, sometimes plan menus, and buy food supplies. They often adjust their menu in response to changes in dietary standards or the availability of fresh ingredients.

As the number of families grows and as the more affluent, 55 and over population increases, demand will grow for restaurants that offer table service and more varied menus—requiring more skilled cooks and chefs.

Hotels, Resorts, and Country Clubs

Hotels, resorts, and country clubs have different types and sizes of kitchens in their facilities. For instance, many hotels, resorts, and country clubs have medium- to large-size restaurants ranging from casual to elegant, as well as offering banquets or other special events. Many hotels also offer room service, coffee shops where baked goods are sold, and weekend buffets in the main dining room. You may even find part-time or seasonal work at popular tourist resort areas as a way to break into the field.

Personal Chef Businesses

The personal chef industry is growing. You may have heard of celebrities such as Oprah and Cher who enjoy the luxury of having a personal chef cook delicious meals for them daily. And many high-ranking politicians employ personal chefs as well, including the president and some governors and mayors. The personal chef movement has recently opened up to include many other people—those who want and are willing to pay for healthy meals on a regular basis. Personal chefs may work for one family and spend time each day in that family's kitchen cooking meals, or they may work for several families and merely drop off food once a week at each family's home. As a personal chef, you may sit down and discuss with clients their food preferences and budget and plan out menus based on that conversation. Your duties may include shopping for the ingredients and cooking and delivering the meals to one or several homes. According to Sharon Odmann, chef owner of Kiyote Cowboy Cookery and Personal Chef Services, a typical personal chef service includes:

- customized menus
- grocery shopping
- meal preparation
- variety of healthful meals
- fresh fruits and vegetables
- top-quality meats and fish
- canola and olive oils
- no added preservatives
- a clean kitchen

Here are just a few examples of the foods that Personal Chef Sharon Odmann serves: braised pork chops with onions, apples, raisins, and dried cranberries; baked snapper with ginger salsa; kung pao chicken; and crab-stuffed pasta shells. To obtain more information about becoming a personal chef, contact one of the organizations for personal chefs listed in Appendix A: the Personal Chef Association or the American Personal Chefs Institute.

Cruise Ships

Some cooks and chefs desire to ride the high seas as a part of their career. Executive Chef Ann Cooper was a chef de partie on the Holland America cruise line early in her career. She says:

If you want to work on a cruise ship, be prepared for a lot of hard work—you will probably be working 16–18 hours a day. It's hard for Americans to get hired on world cruise lines and the pay is very low. However, if you do get hired, you'll get to see wonderful places.

See chapter five for information about a Web site that lists job openings for cooks and chefs aboard cruise ships. Even if it's not a long-term job you'd like to hold, perhaps a year or so at sea would fit into your overall career plan.

Health Spas

If you have a desire to cook healthy or low-calorie meals, joining the kitchen in a health spa may fit your work style. Many popular resorts and health spas offer high-quality, low-fat meals in an elegant setting. While many of the kitchen stations in a health spa kitchen are the same as in any other restaurant kitchen, you will have the opportunity to specialize in healthy cooking with fresh, premium ingredients. You may also get to experiment with many new methods for preparing delicious foods that are low in fat, calories, and cholesterol.

Banquet Halls

Many chefs and cooks are employed by owners of banquet halls, reception halls, party rooms, and hotels to handle special events, such as wedding receptions, political galas, holiday parties, bar mitzvahs, sweet sixteen parties, and corporate parties or meetings. The chefs and cooks who work in such places often prepare and cook large buffets or sit-down meals. The executive chef may be responsible for planning the menus and coordinating the kitchen services needed for each client.

Federal Government

Several cooks, chefs, and cook instructors are needed to work for the federal government in both civilian and military areas. Many job openings are on military bases or are civilian jobs that take place within a military operation. One benefit of working for the military is that you can take advantage of their free training programs and even earn money to put towards a college degree. Are you interested in cooking aboard a navy ship or on a military base in Europe? If so, investigate job opportunities in the federal government. See chapter five for a Web site that will give you more info in this area.

Catering Companies

Working for a catering company can give you valuable culinary experience with a great deal of variety and oftentimes a flexible schedule. Depending on the size and popularity of the catering company, you may be working steady hours every week or you may get several days off in a row in between "gigs," so to speak. Some catering companies specialize in a particular type of food, such as Asian, French, Italian, or kosher. Other catering companies handle large parties or receptions and the work can be similar to working in a banquet hall, preparing appetizers and large buffets. Catering experience can prove useful if you later decide to branch out and create your own catering company. See chapter six for information about starting your own catering company.

Corporate Dining Rooms

In their struggle to retain quality employees, many corporations have opened dining rooms either for all their employees, or just for their executives. These corporate dining rooms can run the gamut from very formal white tablecloth service to a noisy cafeteria. Some corporations also sponsor banquets and special events on a regular basis—there is quite a variety of corporate dining facilities. For example, Chef Mary Cannataro describes the type of dining she offered while working in a corporate dining environment. She says:

> I was the chef/food service manager for a large corporation. Instead of offering the typical cafeteria style, we provided several different stations for people to choose their food from, such as carved meats, pasta, vegetables, and so on; we served between 400–500 people a day.

Grocery Stores/Supermarkets

There is a growing trend for cooks and chefs to find employment in grocery stores preparing take-out meals for consumers who are too busy to cook themselves. Many chefs call this trend "home meal replacement" and deals on ready-to-eat meals are on the rise. While some chefs may think working in a supermarket is beneath them, others are finding it to be an excellent opportunity to shorten their work hours to only 40 per week and to increase their job satisfaction. Some industry insiders have predicted that as many as one in four or even one in three chefs will be working in supermarkets within the next few years, so this market should not be ignored when you are considering your area of specialization within the culinary arts field.

Casual Restaurants

Restaurants that offer casual dining often feature a limited number of easy-to-prepare items, supplemented by short-order specialties and ready-made desserts. Often, one or two cooks prepare all the food with the help of a short-order cook and one or two other kitchen workers. Casual restaurants include most chain restaurants, family-style restaurants, diners, and fast-food restaurants that offer a seating area.

Institutions

Institutions such as schools, industrial cafeterias, hospitals, prisons, and senior living residences employ chefs and cooks to work in their kitchens. These cooks and chefs regularly prepare a large quantity of a limited number of entrees, vegetables, and desserts. Some chefs and cooks also assist in developing menus, directing the work of other kitchen workers, estimating food requirements, and ordering food supplies. Many high schools and hospitals are trying to make institutional food more attractive to students, staff, visitors, and patients to create a more positive image of their establishment.

Chef Geraldine Born, a certified culinary educator at the Pinellas Technical Education Center, says, "many hospitals and nursing homes are improving the quality of their food, and many are moving toward offering catered meals." Indeed, many institutions are decreasing their use of packaged and prepared foods in favor of cooking with fresh ingredients. Chef Mary Cannataro notes an example of the improvement in the quality of institution food service. She says:

> I volunteer once a week to work in the kitchen at a nursing home, where there is an emerging trend to use more fresh ingredients and focus on healthier, more flavorful cooking. Many institutions seem to be moving away from just opening a large can of vegetables and throwing them on a plate.

So the opportunities in institutional kitchens are growing more attractive to many chefs and cooks, who prefer to cook from scratch with raw ingredients.

Chef Born mentions that if you would like to work more reasonable hours in a location near your home, institutional cooking may be a good fit for you. While your specific work shift may vary, the hours are normally no earlier than 5:00 A.M. and no later than 8:00 P.M. So if you work the morning shift, it would not start before 5:00 A.M., and if you work the afternoon/evening shift, it would end by 8:00 P.M. Whereas, in a restaurant kitchen, if you work the evening shift, you may still be cleaning the kitchen at 1:00 A.M.

Retail Bakery and Pastry Shops

Many bakers and pastry makers work in retail bakeries and pastry shops. Frequently, the head pastry chef is also the owner of the shop. Bakeries and pastry shops are often located in or near busy commercial or tourist districts. They provide baked goods ranging from sourdough bread to muffins to delicate crois-sants and elaborate wedding cakes. Most shops open early in the morning to provide baked breakfast items for people rushing off to work. They usually serve coffee and may or may not have a small seating area. Bakery shops may create all baked goods from scratch or they may purchase items that are already partially prepared and just bake them on the premises. In addition to individual shops, small baking and pastry outlets may be found inside large hotels, supermarkets, and office buildings.

Industrial Baking Plants

Industrial or commercial baking involves the large-scale production of breads, cookies, pastries, and frozen doughs using large and sophisticated equipment. Industrial baking plants employ a large number of bakers. According to the American Institute of Baking (AIB), "industrial baking is much more stable than the volatile restaurant and foodservice trade, and wages are nearly always significantly higher." For example, the AIB notes that "many trained industrial bakers with several years of experience and advanced certificates currently earn more than $30,000 per year, with plant level supervisory personnel usually earning in the range of $65,000 to more than $125,000." Industrial bakers normally have a two- or four-year degree in bakery or food science and additional technical experience. The products they bake are sold to supermarkets, bakeries, restaurants, and other baked goods outlets.

FAST-GROWING GEOGRAPHIC LOCATIONS

If you don't mind relocating in your quest for a great job in the culinary arts, there are areas of the country that are growing in their need for food service professionals. These areas include portions of New York, California, Colorado, Florida, Arizona, and Georgia. Several chefs share their insights into where the hottest jobs can be found.

Chef Mary Cannataro in Chicago, Illinois says:

> You should be able to land a good job in any big city. For example, here in Chicago where there seem to be a million restaurants, you still find that new restaurants are opening all the time. You can also look for jobs in small tourist areas that are growing in popularity, such as towns in Montana and Colorado.

Chef Sharon Odmann in Lancaster, Pennsylvania says:

> Find a place that demographically is showing the beginning of growth. Here in Lancaster where I live, the unemployment is very low and there are many jobs available in food service. It's becoming more of a bedroom community for the metropolitan areas. We're experiencing massive growth. New superstores and shopping centers are opening up all the time and popular franchise restaurants are coming into the area.

Chef Timothy Rodgers in Hyde Park, New York, says:

> The best locations for landing a good job in the culinary arts today are mainly in big cities or resort areas, such as New York, Chicago, San Francisco, Los Angeles, Florida, and South Carolina; Utah and Idaho are also growing as resort areas right now.

Many chefs believe new culinary arts professionals have a lot to gain by traveling and working in a variety of kitchens in a variety of places. In addition to the many opportunities available in America for cooks and chefs, jobs in Europe and other countries may appeal to you. Once you gain a solid culinary background, your talents can be put to use just about anywhere in the world.

EDUCATIONAL TRENDS

Culinary arts professionals in many different areas of specialization are increasingly obtaining higher levels of education than they have in the past. Years ago most people learned culinary skills while working their way through the stations in a variety of kitchens, and many did not possess even a high school diploma.

However, today many people have some post-secondary education, ranging from a certificate to a few college courses, an associate degree, or even a bachelor's or master's degree in the culinary arts. Culinary schools across the nation report a steadily increasing enrollment every year. Additionally, many colleges and technical schools are creating new culinary training programs.

Chefs and cooks also may be trained in apprenticeship programs, such as the three-year apprenticeship program administered by local chapters of the American Culinary Federation in cooperation with local employers and junior colleges or vocational education institutions. In addition, some large hotels and restaurants operate their own training programs for cooks and chefs. Most experienced chefs recommend that people who want to become chefs undergo some type of formal training program.

Many post-secondary schools offer hands-on culinary training that is specifically tailored to help students become professional cooks or chefs. See chapter two for detailed information about the many types of training programs that are available in the culinary arts field, and how you can choose the one that's best for you.

THE INSIDE TRACK

Who:	Ann Cooper
What:	Executive Chef at the Putney Inn; Author of the book entitled *A Woman's Place is in the Kitchen*
Where:	Putney, Vermont
How long:	Twenty-five years in the culinary arts industry

Insider's Advice

My advice to people who are considering a culinary arts career is to go work in a restaurant—find a job as an assistant cook in a professional kitchen. You may find out that a good part of working in a professional kitchen is heavy, boring, and repetitive. While there is some good to be said for the rise in celebrity of many chefs in the industry, it can also give newcomers to the field the wrong impression. Think about what you want in your career and investigate different types of employers. In a small restaurant kitchen, you may be able to work side by side with the chef. However, in a large hotel kitchen, you may be working among 70 or 80 people and never even meet the chef. Look at several different eating establishments and ask to work for a day in each of their kitchens to get a feel for the different types of working environments.

Other tips for success in this industry include a good work ethic, determination, and a sense of humor. When you land your first job as a line cook, ask lots of questions, listen closely to the answers, work hard, volunteer for extracurricular activities, and continue to read everything about cooking that you can get your hands on—cookbooks, magazines, professional books, and so on.

Insider's Take on the Future

Research shows that by the year 2007, one out of every four chefs and cooks will work for a grocery store chain. Many grocery stores are in competition with restaurants for consumer dollars in the food and beverage industry. More upscale culinary products are being sold in grocery stores, such as breads, desserts, and salads made from premium ingredients.

Demographic studies show an increase in the number of people over 70. Some of the people in the 70+ age group are moving into extended care facilities. These facilities may include condominiums with price tags in the six or seven figures. Over 400 such facilities were built in Florida in just one year, and many of them have restaurants that serve dinner from 4–7 P.M.

Other evidence of growth in the culinary arts field is the growth of culinary schools and culinary students over the past ten years—it has gone from 60 schools and 6,000 students to 600 schools and 60,000 students.

CHAPTER | 2

This chapter explains the many types of training programs available for becoming a culinary arts professional. You'll find several culinary arts program descriptions from a variety of schools and find tips on how to choose the best school for you.

ALL ABOUT TRAINING PROGRAMS

The importance of culinary training programs and continuing education should not be underestimated if you want to rise to the top of your field. If you are still in high school, you may be able to benefit from culinary programs that students can attend as a part of their academic schedule. If you've already graduated from high school, perhaps you'd like to gain culinary skills in an on-the-job training program by becoming an apprentice. On the other hand, attending a culinary school may be the right choice for you.

There is a tremendous variety of training programs to choose from. Whichever path you take, remember that a chef's training is never complete; there is always more to learn. While you can break into the professional cooking industry without any formal training and work your way up, it could take many years and you may not get the breadth or depth of culinary training that can turn you into a top-notch chef.

Indeed, many reasons exist for attending a culinary school, from learning the basics of cooking, to jump-starting your career, to advancing to a higher-level job. For example, producer Kim O'Donnel, a cooking school graduate, describes the benefits of her culinary education:

> While I was at Peter Kump's New York Cooking School, I developed a more discriminating palate; we would taste 14 different kinds of mustard during one afternoon. I also appreciated seeing the whole process of planning and preparing a dinner for a group of 80 people. From coming up with the ideas, to developing a menu, to preparing 80 lobsters, I had the chance to see all the pieces come together. Plus, the whole concept of teamwork was really impressed on me. If you can't work as part of a team in a kitchen, you'll get fired. I also became extremely organized because we were graded on how well our *mise en place* was organized.

Chef Mike Nipper, another cooking school graduate, shares his experience at a cooking school. He explains:

> The chef I was working for had gone to culinary school and really thought that was the thing to do. So I applied to the New England Culinary Institute in Vermont, and after a rigorous selection process, I was accepted into their two-year program. The program has no breaks—except for one day off at Christmas. The school runs a hotel, bakery, and two restaurants. The students also work at banquets and weddings. We made everything from scratch. When we were assigned to the bakery, we started our day at 3:45 in the morning. The school was very strict. In fact, it was an almost militaristic experience. Your whites had to be pressed, you had to be shaved, and you had to be on time every day. You couldn't miss a day. Missing a day would be like setting yourself back a week. If you missed three days, you would be kicked out of school. It was an incredible experience.

Read on to get a feel for the types of training programs that are available. Remember, there are a lot of options, so carefully weigh the pros and cons of each before selecting one.

Culinary Scoop

What is mise en place? *Mise en place* refers to preparing your kitchen station with all equipment and ingredients needed for your shift.

TYPES OF TRAINING PROGRAMS

You can take several different routes to getting the culinary arts training you need. Below are descriptions of the major types of training programs that are available for all experience levels ranging from high school diplomas to bachelor's degrees.

High School Preparation

If you haven't yet completed high school, you can take courses that will help you to prepare for entering the culinary arts field. First of all, make sure that you have a handle on basic skills such as reading comprehension, writing, computer literacy, and mathematics.

To prepare in a more in-depth way, ask your guidance counselor or home economics instructor if your high school is involved in any special culinary training programs. Here is a program that has gained national attention:

Careers Through Culinary Arts Program

The Careers Through Culinary Arts Program was founded by Richard Grausman in 1990 in New York City. Since then, the program has grown quickly—it is now active in seven cities and over 200 high schools in:

* Philadelphia, Pennsylvania
* Washington, DC
* Los Angeles, California
* Chicago, Illinois
* Phoenix, Arizona
* Norfolk, Virginia
* New York City, New York

This innovative, hands-on program allows high school students to obtain practical training in the culinary arts. At the end of the program, each student who is eligible may enter a cooking contest to compete for thousands of dollars in scholarships to post-secondary culinary schools. Students may qualify for the program if they have at least a C+ grade point average and can demonstrate significant ability in the kitchen. Internships are also included in several high schools. You can contact the Careers Through Culinary Arts Program by calling 212-873-2434 (additional contact information is in Appendix A).

By building a strong educational foundation while still in high school, you'll increase your chances of succeeding in the next phase of your culinary training, whether it's an apprenticeship, certificate, associate degree, or bachelor's degree.

Apprenticeship Programs

The history of apprenticeship programs in the culinary arts is long indeed. Americans adopted the idea from the French system—a system that's been used to train new kitchen workers for centuries. The most widely known apprenticeships in America are sponsored by the American Culinary Federation.

American Culinary Federation Apprenticeships

The American Culinary Federation Educational Institute (ACFEI) offers a formal apprenticeship program that offers practical experience to people wishing to build their culinary careers through paid on-the-job training. The program requires apprentices to work for 6,000 hours (three years) under the supervision of a chef in a professional kitchen.

Apprentices must also attend school part-time while they are serving as an apprentice; 192 classroom hours per year are needed. In most cases, you can take courses at a local community or technical college one or two days a week throughout the three years you are an apprentice. While serving as an apprentice, you'll gain experience working in these different kitchen stations:

- breakfast
- vegetable
- broiler
- sauté
- baking
- garde manger
- pantry
- sauce
- soup
- butcher
- pastry

You'll also learn about developing recipes, designing menus, purchasing ingredients, and budgeting food and labor costs. Courses in sanitation and safety are also required, preferably at the beginning of your training program.

To enter the apprenticeship program, you must be at least 17 years of age and possess a high school diploma or its equivalent. You'll find a list at the end of chapter three of the nearly 80 different ACFEI apprenticeship programs located throughout the nation. Some local chapters have waiting lists of more than a year long, so if you are interested, contact the ACFEI's national office as soon as possible to find out more about apprenticeship programs in your region (see Appendix A for contact information).

Short-Term Culinary Courses and Seminars

Many short-term training programs or seminars lasting even a day or a weekend can offer helpful culinary training in a particular type of cooking or baking. While short-term programs are not a substitute for solid experience and a training program lasting months or years, they can offer productive sessions to complement a more in-depth training program for the aspiring chef.

Baking Courses

The American Institute of Baking (AIB) sponsors a School of Baking that offers students advanced training for positions in the baking and allied industries. Seminars and short courses offered by the AIB are held during the year, both in Kansas and in locations throughout the United States and a number of other countries. These short courses offer bakers and pastry culinarians an opportunity to update their technical knowledge and sharpen their bakery skills. An annual calendar of events is available on their Web site at http://www.aibonline.org. Or you can contact the AIB for details about their short-term courses and certification seminars—their address and phone number appear in Appendix A.

Another example of short-term baking courses is found at the California Culinary Academy in San Francisco. This culinary school offers weekend demonstration classes, such as Fabulous French Pastry, Fancy Cookies, and other baking courses. For example, in Basic Cakes II, you'd learn how to make light cakes using the foaming method—angel food cakes, chiffon cakes, and sponge roll cakes. Or you might want to take a course entitled French Pastry Basics, in which you'd learn about making croissants, fruit tarts, cream puffs, eclairs, and pastry creams.

Cooking Courses Abroad

Perhaps you'd like to travel to another country to take a short culinary course or workshop. Several opportunities are available to you. For instance, you could attend the Ritz Escoffier Ecole de Gastronomie Française in Paris for a week-long cooking course about French cuisine. If you have the time and money to stay longer, perhaps you'd like the six-week cooking program. If so, you'd be eligible to take a practical exam and get the César Ritz Diploma. Other programs at the school include a 12-week advanced cooking course, a one-, six-, or 12-week French pastry course, a 30-week grand diplôme in cuisine and pastry, and many varied continuing education courses. For more information, contact the Ritz Escoffier Ecole de Gastronomie Française at 800-966-5758.

Another prestigious French cooking school is Le Cordon Bleu, which offers classes in Paris, London, Tokyo, North America, and Sydney. They offer a range of culinary courses and programs, including Le Grand Diplôme Le Cordon Bleu, Master Chef Catering Program, and the International Culinary Summer Abroad program. To get more information, contact Le Cordon Bleu, Inc., at 800-457-CHEF.

Studying or working abroad is a dream that many culinary students have when they first embark on their training. And it is a dream than some do achieve in the course of their career. Even if the experience lasts only a short time, it is an experience that will never be forgotten.

Many other opportunities exist to take short-term courses or seminars in the culinary arts from a variety of schools, associations, and other programs. Contact the professional associations found in Appendix A to get information on programs they offer. You can also check your daily newspaper for culinary competitions or demonstrations from well-known chefs in your local region. Some community college programs or other post-secondary schools may also offer seminars or workshops for aspiring chefs. See chapter three for a list of colleges, technical schools, and institutes that offer culinary training programs—they often sponsor short-term classes or day-long seminars.

Certificate Programs

Certificate programs normally range from several weeks to several months to one year or more, depending on the school offering the program. Many community colleges, vocational schools, culinary institutes, and a few universities offer certificate programs in culinary arts. You may decide to explore different areas of specialization in the culinary arts or delve further into topics that interest you by completing one or more certificate programs throughout your culinary career.

You'll want to investigate several schools to find the program that is best for you. The directory listed in chapter three is a great place to start your training program search. Select several schools from the list and contact them to find out if they offer a certificate program and to request a brochure or catalog. Then carefully read all the certificate materials you receive from each school.

You should also speak to an instructor or guidance counselor at the schools you are considering to find out if the culinary arts certificate they offer is a good match for you. There may be more than one certificate offered by a school that falls under the general heading of *Culinary Arts*, so you need to examine each certificate program carefully before enrolling. For example, will the certificate focus on baking or restaurant management rather than cooking? You need to find out what is taught in each certificate program before you apply. Read the course descriptions carefully to find out if the majority of the courses include hands-on learning in a kitchen environment. Most certificate programs require that applicants have a high school diploma or its equivalent before beginning the certificate program.

An example of a typical culinary arts certificate training program is listed below to give you an idea of what you can expect to find in a similar training program near you. This training program is offered at a community college in Illinois. District residents pay $43 per credit hour. Out-of-district residents pay $210 per credit hour, and out-of-state students pay $253 per credit hour.

Sample Baking Certificate Program	
Course Name	**Number of Credit Hours**
Introduction to Professional Food Service	3
Applied Food Service Sanitation	1
Baking I	4
Advanced Pastry	4
Total Credits Required for Certificate:	**12**

It is typical for programs to require regular attendance and an academic average of a "C" or higher (2.0 GPA) to be eligible to receive a certificate upon completion of the program.

Certificate programs vary in content and length depending on the school and the state in which the program is offered. For instance, take a look at the certificate program in culinary arts shown below. This one is offered at a community college in Texas and is much longer than the one listed above. This certificate program requires a total of 45 credit hours. The full-time cost of tuition per year for county residents is $650; for state residents outside the county, it is $1,030; and for out-of-state residents, it is approximately $2,140. Part-time tuition varies according to the course load.

Sample Baking/Pastry Certificate Program	
Course Name	**Number of Credit Hours**
Food Service Safety and Sanitation	3
Breads and Rolls or Elementary Bakery Training	3
Entry Level Cake Decorating	2
Business Mathematics	3
Breads and Rolls or Elementary Bakery Training	3
Pies, Tarts, Tea Cakes, and Cookies	3
Bakery Operations and Management	3
Supervision for Hospitality Services	3
Laminated Doughs, Pate-A-Choux and Donuts	3
Advanced Pastry Shop Training I	3
Cooperative Work Experience	4
Introduction to Speech Communication **or** Composition I	3
Advanced Pastry Shop Training II	3
Cooperative Work Experience	4
Food and Hospitality Service Elective	2
Total Credits Required for Certificate:	**45**

In addition to certificate programs focused solely on baking, there are programs with a cooking emphasis and those with a combined cooking and baking emphasis. For example, the Academy of Culinary Arts at the Indiana University of Pennsylvania (IUP) has a culinary arts certificate program that includes courses in both baking and cooking. The 16-month training program lasts four semesters, including an externship. One benefit of their program is that graduates of the culinary arts certificate program are guaranteed admission, along with 42 transfer credits, into the IUP's Hotel, Restaurant and Institutional Management bachelor of science degree program.

So you can see there are a variety of certificate programs available to culinary arts students. Your choice of program is a big decision, so be sure to read *How to Choose the Training Program That's Best for You*, later in this chapter. Perhaps you want to obtain an associate degree instead of a certificate; if so, there are plenty of associate degrees you can choose from—read on to find out more about this popular option.

Advice from a Culinary Student

"When you are in cooking school, the two main words are 'Yes, chef.' Do what your chef tells you to do as quickly and cheerfully as possible."
Jennifer McAllister, a student in the Pastry and Baking program at Peter Kump's New York Cooking School.

Associate Degrees

An associate degree program's length of study for full-time students is normally two academic years (four semesters), although some schools offer accelerated programs in which you can complete an associate degree in as little as 15 months. Accelerated programs normally require you to attend classes for more hours each day than in regular programs and to take courses during the summer. Entrance requirements for most associate degree programs include a high school diploma or its equivalent. Some programs require students to take entrance and placement exams prior to enrolling in classes, and admission to some culinary institutes' associate degree programs is very competitive. You may need to write an essay describing your interest and background in the culinary arts and provide letters of reference from two or three people. And for some programs, experience working in a professional kitchen is required or favorably looked on by the admissions committee. It never hurts to have a little practical experience.

There are different types of associate degrees you can earn, such as associate of arts, associate of science, associate of specialized technology, and associate of applied science. However, the most common in the culinary arts field is the associate of occupational science degree, commonly known as the A. O. S. degree. Most of the top-ranked private culinary schools in America offer the A. O. S. degree; for instance, the Culinary Institute of America, Johnson & Wales University, and the

New England Culinary Institute. Executive Chef Ann Cooper, author of *A Woman's Place Is in the Kitchen*, graduated from the Culinary Institute of America with an A. O. S. degree. She says, "I left the CIA with a strong sense of professionalism and a passion for the craft."

Although culinary arts associate degree programs vary, students usually spend much of their time learning to prepare and cook food through actual practice. In a typical program, you may learn to bake, broil, sauté, grill, and otherwise prepare and cook food, and to use and care for kitchen utensils and equipment. In addition to hands-on cooking and baking, many associate degree programs include courses in planning menus, determining portion size, maintaining standards of sanitation and safety, controlling food costs, purchasing food supplies in quantity, selecting and storing food, using leftover food to minimize waste, and managing a staff.

Since associate degree programs vary, be sure to read all college materials carefully before you apply to a program. You should also speak to an instructor or guidance counselor at the school you are considering to find out if the culinary arts associate degree it offers is a good match for you. Some programs emphasize training to become a restaurant manager or institutional food service manager rather than a culinary arts professional who cooks or bakes.

The courses required for a culinary arts major in a typical associate degree training program are listed below to give you an idea of what you can expect. This is a program that leads to an associate of occupational science degree in culinary arts at a proprietary institution in California; it is an 18-month full-time program. Seventy-eight credit hours are needed to complete this program. The tuition is $16,728 for the first year and $13,102 for the second year for both residents and nonresidents.

Associate of Occupational Science Degree

Course Title	Number of Credit Hours
Safety/Sanitation	2
Food Science	2
Skill Lab I	2
Skill Lab II	2
Fundamentals of Garde Manger	2
Culinary Arts Survey	4
Practical Kitchen: Prep	2
Food Industry Software	2
Baking Skills I	2
Purchasing and Kitchen Management	3
Foods of the Americas	2
Butchery Lab	2
Principles of European Cuisine	3
Breakfast Cookery	2
Principles of Asian Cuisine	3
Hospitality Management I	4
Wine Appreciation	2
Mid-Level Competency Exams	1
Academy Tavern	2
Hospitality Management II	4
A La Carte Kitchen I	2
Food and Beverage Cost Control	2
Wine and Food Affinities	2
Baking Skills II	2
Fundamentals of Table Service	2
Intermediate Garde Manger	2
Practical Kitchen Management	2
A La Carte Kitchen II	2
Nutrition	2
Final Competency Exams	1
Externship	11
Total Credit Hours Required for Degree:	**78**

While no two associate degree programs are going to be exactly alike, there are some similarities. For instance, most associate degree programs will require hands-on cooking classes where students learn and practice knife handling skills, the basics of how to make sauces and stocks, and food sanitation and safety. Many programs also include baking courses and management courses. Take a look at another sample associate degree program listed below to find the similarities between it and the above program. This is an associate of occupational studies degree offered by a private institution in Arizona. The total tuition for this 15-month accelerated A. O. S. degree program is approximately $16,150 for both residents and nonresidents.

Associate of Occupational Science Degree	
Course Title	**Number of Credit Hours**
Basic Culinary Arts	10
Saucier	4
Meat Fabrication	4
Kitchen Management	.5
Culinary French	.5
Restaurant Operations	4
Baking	4
Catering/Garde Manger	4
A La Carte	4
Management and Human Resources	5
Nutrition	4
Advanced Cuisine	4
Advanced Baking and Pastry	4
Wines and Spirits	3
Purchasing	2
Show Pieces	4
Advanced Operations	4
Student Restaurant	4
Externship	9
Total Credit Hours Required for Degree:	**78**

If you want a training program that is longer and more in-depth than an associate degree, then a bachelor's degree may be just what you're looking for. While there are only a few schools that currently offer bachelor's degrees in the culinary arts, you can find schools that offer related bachelor's degrees in the broader fields of hospitality and restaurant management. These programs may be helpful to aspiring chefs who want to own and manage their own restaurant some day.

Bachelor's Degrees

The bachelor's degree program combines courses in a specific major with general education courses in a four-year curriculum at a college or university. Some students complete one or two years of general education or liberal arts courses at a community college and then transfer to a four-year college or university to obtain a bachelor's degree. There are several types of bachelor's degrees available— the most common are the bachelor of arts and the bachelor of science.

The bachelor of science degree with a major in culinary arts, restaurant management, food service, or hospitality may be what you're looking for. While a bachelor's degree is certainly not required to become a successful chef (most chefs do not have one), it may be useful if you have a desire to combine your culinary skills with management skills. As of this writing, there are very few bachelor's degree programs that focus primarily on hands-on cooking or baking. Johnson & Wales University is the first school in the country to offer both associate and bachelor's degrees in Baking & Pastry Arts and Culinary Arts. The Culinary Institute of America offers a Bachelor of Professional Studies degree program—the first 21 months are the same as the associate degree; the last 17 months include courses on marketing, finance, gastronomy, management, communications, history, language, and culture.

Additionally, the New England Culinary Institute started offering a bachelor's degree in Service and Management in 1993. New York University offers a bachelor of science degree in Food Studies or Food and Restaurant Management. It is the only school in America that offers a food-related bachelor's, master's, and doctorate degree. The Chef John Folse Culinary Institute at Nicholls State University in Louisiana is the first state-supported university to offer a bachelor of science degree in culinary arts; this program allows students to earn an associate of science degree while they are working toward the bachelor of science degree.

Many culinary professionals who decide to enroll in bachelor's degree programs want to focus on restaurant management, institutional food service management, or hospitality management. These programs tend to focus more on business and financial courses than on cooking and baking, at least at the upper-division level. Choosing which training program is right for you is highly personal, so don't be put off from getting a bachelor's degree in culinary arts just because most cooks and chefs don't have one. If your plans include teaching or managing a restaurant or food service institution as well as cooking, then a bachelor's degree may be a big plus.

The following list of courses will give you an idea of what the requirements are for a culinary arts major in a bachelor's degree program. The courses listed below are offered at a university in Louisiana. Electives, which are frequently required for a degree, are not listed. Annual tuition for 12 credit hours and over is approximately $1,068 for in-state residents and $2,490 for nonresidents.

Bachelor of Science Degree: Culinary Arts Courses Required for Major	
Course Title	**Number of Credit Hours**
Culinary Development and History	3
Culinary Foundation	3
Meat Fabrication	2
Institutional Kitchen I	2
Institutional Kitchen II	2
Principles of Food & Beverage Service	3
A La Carte I	2
Garde Manger I	2
Food, Beverage, and Labor Cost Control	3
Culinary Arts Externship	3
Baking I	2
Cajun/Creole Cuisine	2
Food Service Inventory, Selection, Procurement, and Control	3
Beverage Operations	3
Facility Layout and Design	3
Menu Design, Integration, and Promotion	3
Culinary Arts Senior Externship	3
Total Credits Required for Major:	**44**
Total Credits Required for Degree:	**130**

For this program, you would also need to take Nutrition, Food Science, and Supervision courses, although they fall outside of the major. The courses that make up the rest of the degree consist of a mixture of electives and required courses; the ratio of this mixture varies among schools. However, for a bachelor's degree you'll most likely be required to take a variety of general education courses in fields such as the natural sciences, social sciences, mathematics, history, English, fine arts, and communications. You'll also have several elective courses to choose from, many in the culinary arts, business management, or sciences. All of these options are clearly spelled out in each school's catalog, so read the information carefully.

The entrance requirements are normally more competitive for a bachelor's degree program than for shorter training programs. Generally, you will need: high school diploma or its equivalent (GED); satisfactory scores on the SAT, ACT, or other placement exams; a high-quality written essay; positive references; and an acceptable high school GPA. You have to analyze your current financial situation, along with your future career goals, to decide if a bachelor's degree is right for you. Before you make a final decision on what length and type of culinary training program to attend, be sure to check out chapter four's info on financial aid. You don't want a lack of funds to stop you from pursuing a four-year degree—you may be able to afford more college training than you think.

Kitchen Uniform

Cooks and chefs in professional kitchens normally wear a standard uniform consisting of the following:

- white double-breasted jacket
- toque blanche (white hat)
- checkered pants
- apron
- side towel
- neckerchief
- hard-toed shoes

HOW TO CHOOSE THE TRAINING PROGRAM THAT'S BEST FOR YOU

Since there are so many different training programs, it can be a challenge to find the one that is best for you. The first step is to evaluate your current lifestyle and financial situation. Do you need to remain close to home, or could you pack up and move to another state to attend school? If you want to stay in your local area, the choice of which program to attend may be easier—because there won't be as many to choose from. If you're willing to relocate, you may have to spend a little more time evaluating a wide range of schools. In either case, you'll need to start contacting schools to request information about their programs.

You should always confirm that each school currently offers culinary arts courses. Ask to speak to a guidance or admissions counselor or to someone in the culinary arts department to get detailed information about the programs offered by each school. Request a school catalog and whatever brochures they have about the school and its programs. Read this information carefully when you receive it, especially the fine print in the college catalog. You want to find out exactly what courses are required for your program, how much it will cost, and how long it will last.

If possible, arrange to visit the schools you are considering, so you can speak to a guidance counselor, in person, at each one. These counselors are trained to help you identify your needs and decide if their school will meet those needs. Here's what you can do to prepare for an on-campus visit:

- Contact the office of admissions to request an appointment to visit the campus. Some schools may conduct open houses or give tours of their campus. If so, find out when they occur so you can attend.
- If classes are in session, ask if you can observe a culinary class in action.
- For schools that have a student-run restaurant, find out if and when you can dine there.
- If you have extra time, visit the campus library, bookstore, cafeteria, and the building(s) where culinary classes are held.
- Strike up conversations with students on campus to get inside information about the school.

Be prepared to ask questions about the school, the campus, and the surrounding community, including extracurricular activities, work opportunities, and anything else you don't find explained in the promotional brochures.

Application Tips from Admissions Directors

- Call the school to find out when the next program starts, then apply at least a month or two prior to make sure you have time to complete all the requirements before the program begins. Apply as early as you can.

- Complete an application and submit high school or GED transcripts and any copies of SAT, ACT, or other test scores used for admission. If you haven't taken these tests, you may need to do so.

- If you get a request for high school transcripts from the admissions office when you get your application, make sure you send them right away.

- Make an appointment as soon as possible to take any placement tests that are required.

- Pay your tuition and fees before the deadline. Enrollment is not complete until you have paid all fees by the date specified on your registration form. If fees are not paid by the deadline, your classes may be canceled.

- If you are hoping to receive financial aid, complete the financial aid application as early as you can.

- Find out early in the application process if you must provide any medical history forms, such as immunization records.

Ask the Right Questions

After you visit several schools and narrow your choices down to two or three schools, the next step is to ask tough questions about each program, so you can make the final selection. Here are some important questions you should ask about each school you are considering to see if it measures up to your standards. Following the list of questions, you'll find sample answers that you should receive or other considerations that you should look for in a prospective school before selecting it as your first choice.

Questions to Ask

What requirements will I need to fulfill?

Is the school accredited?

What are the qualifications of the faculty?

What will the program cost?

Does the school have practice kitchens? If so, how many?

Does the school sponsor a restaurant, café, or bakery?

What type of externships does the school offer?

What type of job placement assistance is available?

What is the school's student-instructor ratio?

When are classes scheduled?

Is the campus environment suitable?

Does the school offer child-care facilities?

What requirements will I need to fulfill?

Check with each school you are considering to find out what its specific entrance requirements are—they vary from school to school. For instance, you may be required to do any one or more of the following:

- write a personal essay stating why you are seeking admission
- provide the names and phone numbers for two or more personal references
- provide letters of reference from previous employers, instructors, or industry professionals
- take English, math, or science placement tests
- take and achieve a certain score on the SAT or ACT if you have not already taken them in high school
- have a certain level GPA from high school

If you feel that you won't have any trouble meeting the entrance requirements for your targeted schools, then you're all set. If one of the schools you are considering has an entrance requirement that you think you may not meet, call an admissions counselor and discuss your particular case with her or him. Many schools will at least offer some type of remedial help, so students can meet the requirement in the future.

Is the school accredited?

The school you choose to attend should be accredited if it has been in operation for over five years. Accreditation is a rigorous and complex process that schools undergo voluntarily to ensure that they offer a high-quality education to their students. It is an indication that a culinary program meets recognized standards regarding course content, facilities, and quality of instruction. Therefore, if a school you're considering is not accredited, ask an admissions counselor why and find out if the school is currently seeking accreditation. Be aware that if the school you choose is not accredited, then you cannot get financial aid through any of the government programs. (See chapter four for more information on how to obtain financial aid.)

The names of the accrediting agencies for the school you're interested in will probably be plainly printed in the school's general catalog because most schools are proud of their accredited status. If you can't locate the information in a school's printed materials, call the school and ask for the name(s) of its accrediting agency or agencies. Many schools are accredited by more than one accrediting agency. For example, the culinary arts program at Delgado Community College in New Orleans, Louisiana, is accredited by both the Southern Association of Colleges and Schools and by the American Culinary Federation Education Institute (ACFEI). The ACFEI has only been accrediting culinary programs for a short time, so don't be disheartened if the school you're interested in has not received this distinction yet. However, the ACFEI has accredited almost 100 training programs in America, and that number keeps rising every year as more and more schools seek to achieve this important accreditation. See Appendix A to get contact information for applicable accrediting agencies, including the ACFEI.

What are the qualifications of the faculty?

Faculty members should have extensive experience as culinary arts professionals and instructors. Some faculty members hold associate or bachelor's degrees in culinary arts or a related area. For example, many culinary arts instructors possess the A. O. S. degree from a culinary institute. Some faculty members should also hold professional certifications from a professional association. For instance, many chef instructors have the letters CCE after their name because they possess the professional designation of *Certified Culinary Educator* from the American Culinary Federation. See chapter six for more information about the many different certification programs that are available.

Some faculty members are cookbook authors, practicing chefs, or owners of a restaurant. Look for instructors who have extensive experience in the culinary industry and who have held a wide variety of roles in professional kitchens.

In a four-year college or university, you can expect the majority of professors to hold advanced degrees. In shorter programs, you'll find more instructors who are currently practicing as sous chefs, chefs, or executive chefs who may not have formal education but are well-known in their area of specialization. In all types of training programs, however, the faculty should be accessible to students for individual conferences or meetings when necessary.

What will the program cost?

Tuition varies according to many factors: the length of the program, the area in which the school is located, and whether the school is a private or public institution. For public institutions, tuition costs often depend on if you are a resident of the state or county in which you are attending school. You should figure out how much each program that you are considering will cost. If the tuition is not listed in the college's course catalog, call the school to find out what its current rates are. As you can see from the tuition costs listed in the sample programs appearing previously in this chapter (certificate, associate, and bachelor's), there is quite a range of costs for completing a culinary arts training program. Several private culinary institutes charge students from $10,000 to $25,000 for a culinary certificate or an associate degree. However, financial aid is available and some schools help students to secure part-time jobs to help offset tuition costs. For example, the Western Culinary Institute in Portland, Oregon assists students in finding part-time work during the school year.

Don't forget to include the following items when figuring out how much each school will cost: admission fees, textbooks, knives and other cooking supplies, uniforms, rent, food (find out if you can eat for free in a student dining room—many programs offer this perk), and transportation. If a school is located near where you live, you may be able to save money on parking and gasoline by walking or taking a bus. After you create an estimate of the total costs for each school you are considering, you can add that information to your pros and cons list. However, before you rule out a school because of its high cost, read chapter four on financial aid.

Does the school have practice kitchens? If so, how many?

You'll need to get some hands-on experience in an actual kitchen, so you can practice the cooking and baking principles you learn during lecture classes. If possible, ask to visit a school's kitchens while a class is in session, so you can observe how the students interact with the instructor. Also check to see if there is ample workspace for everyone to get their work done in each class, or if students must rotate in order to get to a stovetop or oven. Is the equipment new or outdated? You can gather a lot of information simply by viewing and comparing the practice kitchens in several schools—how do they stack up against each other? Here are some examples of equipment that is typically found in practice kitchens:

- broilers
- convection ovens
- deep fryers
- freezers
- griddles
- grills
- grinders
- meat choppers
- microwave ovens
- mixers (table and standing)
- ovens
- preparation tables
- ranges
- refrigerators (walk-in and upright)
- rotisseries
- sausage makers
- slicing machines
- steam cabinets
- steam kettles
- tilting skillets
- woks

Does the school sponsor a restaurant, café, or bakery?

Many schools with culinary arts training programs sponsor their own restaurants or bakeries that are open to students, faculty, and visitors, and sometimes to the general public. These restaurants give students a chance to get real-world experience under the tutelage of a chef instructor. For example, the Florida Culinary Institute runs Café Protégé, an elegant, on-site restaurant that is open to the public. Students work alongside chefs to find out firsthand how to meet production goals in an efficient manner. Some cooking schools have even more than one restaurant. Indeed, the Culinary Institute of America boasts four student-staffed restaurants on their Hyde Park campus in New York.

Many programs offer training in front-of-the-house positions as well. For example, a course at the California Culinary Academy covers the fundamentals of table service in a restaurant. In this course, students learn the basics of preparing, carving, saucing, and plating poultry, meat, and game at tableside. Students also practice proper serving techniques, grooming, and sanitation while serving guests in the school's restaurant. This experience can prove to be very helpful if you one day hope to open your own restaurant, or if you decide to move into restaurant management.

What type of externships does the school offer?

Externships offer students the chance to work in a restaurant, hotel, or institutional kitchen to gain practical culinary experience. Externships are also known as internships, and they may be paid or unpaid positions. Many schools require culinary students to complete a specified number of hours in an externship at an approved commercial food service establishment. For example, students in the Academy of Culinary Arts at the Indiana University of Pennsylvania are required to complete 450 hours in an externship that is approved by the Academy. The externship may be located near the university, in the student's hometown, or in a faraway exotic place.

You'll want to find an externship that is in line with your career goals. Chef Sharon Odmann describes her externship:

> I did my externship at the Days Inn hotel where I was already working as banquet chef. I created intense fresh buffets every day for happy hour. The food included fresh and smoked salmon and was placed on mirrors—management put a lot of money into the buffets. In addition to doing buffets, I worked the hot line, and I felt good about myself because working the line is very hard work.

Ask to see a list of places where students have completed externships from each school you are considering. Then compare the lists. Do you see several establishments on the list that you would be interested in? Choose your externship carefully because it may lead to your first full-time position after graduation. If you want to specialize in baked goods, then look for positions in which you could work under an esteemed or influential pastry chef. Perhaps classic French cuisine is where your interests lie. If so, find out if the schools you are considering can help you find an externship in a classic French restaurant. Look for a school that offers flexibility in which externship you choose. If you need to switch gears midway through an externship, make sure your school will approve the change. Kim O'Donnel, a graduate of Peter Kump's New York Cooking School, shares her externship experience:

> I decided to go to a well-known restaurant in Philadelphia for a paid externship. I only stayed for three weeks because I hated it. It wasn't gratifying because it wasn't about the food, it was about money. I left and went over to a nonprofit kitchen that prepared food for home-bound people with HIV. It was so much more fulfilling, and even though it was an unpaid externship, I loved it.

What type of job placement assistance is available?

Most schools offer job placement assistance, so if you find a school that doesn't, screen that school very carefully. Many culinary programs will proudly quote their rate of success at placing graduates in jobs, indeed; you'll often find schools that claim 90%–100% of their graduates have obtained jobs within six months of graduation. For example, the Pennsylvania Institute of Culinary Arts states that out of the 2,168 graduates available for placement between the May 1993 and March 1998 graduating classes, 98% were placed in the field. Now that's some record!

Since the field of culinary arts is growing so quickly, you shouldn't have trouble finding a job upon graduation. The question is, what kind of a job will you find? Look for schools whose graduates get job offers from the type of restaurants or institutions you want to work for. You can ask a representative of each school if she or he has names of companies who have hired that school's alumni. Additionally, find out how many job offers each student typically gets upon graduation. Some schools boast that their graduates choose from among four or five job offers.

What is the school's student-instructor ratio?

The student-instructor ratio is a statistic that shows the average number of students assigned to one instructor in a classroom or lab. It's important that the student-instructor ratio is low because your education may suffer if classrooms are too crowded. This is especially true in labs, where students need to interact with their instructor while cooking or baking. According to the Accrediting Council for Independent Colleges and Schools, a reasonable student-instructor ratio for skills training is 30 students to one teacher in a lecture setting and 15 students to one teacher in a laboratory instruction setting. At some schools, the ratio is even better than the ACICS recommends. For instance, the New England Culinary Institute advertises that they have cut their class size down to seven students to one instructor to increase the quality of each student's education.

When are classes scheduled?

Find out if the schools you're considering offer a mixture of day, weekend, and evening classes. If you are working in a professional kitchen while attending school, you'll need to find a school that offers a flexible schedule of classes to accommodate your work schedule. Or perhaps you want to attend school full-time; if so, you should have that option. Jennifer McAllister, a student in the Pastry and Baking program at Peter Kump's New York Cooking School, says:

> The start dates for entering the baking program here at Peter Kump's are very flexible. The school offers a part- and full-time day program and a part-time evening program. I chose the full-time day program, so I am in class from 9–4 (with a half-hour lunch). I wanted total immersion, and this program gave me the maximum number of hours.

Is the campus environment suitable for your needs?

When you visit each school, determine how the campus feels to you. Is it too big? Too small? Too quiet? Is the campus in a bustling city or rural community? Is it easily accessible? Do you need to rely on public transportation to get there? Are there student residences on campus? Select a school that has a campus environment that meets your needs.

Does the school offer child-care facilities?

This may or may not be of concern to you. If it is, you'll want to tour the child-care facilities and interview the people who work in the child-care center to see if the care is appropriate for your children.

Advice for Culinary Students

Chef Geraldine Born, a certified culinary educator and advanced culinary skills instructor at Pinellas Technical Education Center, encourages her students to:

- Enter culinary competitions; the American Culinary Federation (ACF) sponsors several regional student competitions every year. It's good experience.

- Get involved as a student member in your local chapter of the ACF.

- Read the annual Restaurant Issue of *Gourmet* Magazine to find out about leading restaurants in the nation; use the guide to look for exciting places to work after you graduate.

- Travel. Go work in other states. Get exposure to new experiences.

Once you select the training program that's best for you, it's time to begin investigating financial aid. See chapter four for an inside look at the financial aid process and to find out if there are any culinary arts scholarships for which you would be eligible.

Who:	Timothy Rodgers, CEC, CHE (Certified Executive Chef, Certified Hospitality Educator)
What:	Team Leader for Curriculum and Instruction, Meat and Garde Manger at the Culinary Institute of America
Where:	Hyde Park, New York
How long:	Twenty-two years in the culinary arts field

Insider's Advice

If you want to go to the top, there's a five-year plan you can adopt. It's an aggressive plan. But I suggest that you find someone who is the absolute best at what they do, in a particular city, anywhere in the world. You make a one-year commitment to that person and you give it your all. You do whatever is asked of you. Just pour yourself into it. After your one-year commitment (and you always make it clear that it's a one-year commitment), you move to a different city. Then you do it all over again, only you have to find someone who has a different style or a different type of operation from the first one. Do that for five years, moving to a new place each year.

As long as you're associating yourself with the best in the industry at each stage, then you can go anywhere. This way, you build up your life experiences by living in new environments, meeting new people, and adapting to new situations. An added benefit is that your resume is filled with a history of working with top-notch people. I think that this five-year plan is much better than going through a formal apprenticeship program in America because as far as I'm concerned, there aren't many good ones in this country. There are some, however. For example, the Greeenbriar Hotel—they have a formal three-year apprenticeship program. But there are few formal apprenticeship programs that I think are the way to go.

Resist the temptation to become a chef too soon. Once you're the chef, the learning opportunities become fewer and fewer. So another piece of advice is "Don't fall into the temptation to follow the buck." Working for low pay at the beginning is an investment in your future if you get the opportunity to work for the best people in the industry. If you want to get to the top, start at the bottom. If you jump to the middle too soon, that's where you're going to end up.

Insider's Take on the Future

Personally, I see a big split in the future of culinary arts—I see it going in two different directions. In one direction, I see a trend toward a lot of mediocrity and low-end convenience food and in the other direction a trend toward fine dining, high-end, gourmet type scenarios.

These trends are occurring mainly in restaurants, but there is a new trend called HMR (Home Meal Replacement) that is coming up pretty strong. It hasn't been clearly defined as of yet but it's something between a grocery store and a restaurant. You can take food away hot and ready to eat, or food that is ready to be cooked, or ingredients to cook yourself at home. Additionally, the personal chef trend is growing in popularity. It's similar to home meal solutions, where a chef will sit down and talk to a family and set them up for a week's worth of meals at a time. On a Saturday or Sunday morning, the chef delivers a week's work of meals that are ready to heat and serve.

CHAPTER | 3

This chapter contains a directory of public and private schools, colleges, institutes, and universities that offer culinary arts training programs. For each program, you'll find the school name, address, phone number, and, where available, the fax and Internet address, so you can contact each school directly to get more information and application forms. At the end of this directory is a list of apprenticeship programs sponsored by the American Culinary Federation.

DIRECTORY OF CULINARY ARTS TRAINING PROGRAMS

The number of culinary training programs in America is increasing every year. The schools listed in this directory offer certificates, diplomas, associate degrees, or bachelor's degrees in culinary arts or baking and pastry arts. To find out exactly what type of training each school provides, call or write to ask for brochures and course catalogs. Some schools may offer their culinary arts courses under another heading, such as hospitality, food service, or restaurant management.

The schools in this chapter are listed in alphabetical order within each state, so you can quickly locate schools in your area. The specific schools included in this chapter are not endorsed or recommended by

LearningExpress; they are intended to help you begin your search for an appropriate school by offering a representative listing of accredited schools in each state. Obviously, not all of the culinary arts programs in the country could be listed here, but this representative listing should get you started. The training programs these schools offer range from a 12-credit hour certificate course to an associate degree to a bachelor's degree and beyond. Therefore, you should contact each school to find out exactly what type of culinary arts training they offer.

At the end of this directory is a list of apprenticeship programs sponsored by the American Culinary Federation. The programs are categorized by state; if you are interested in applying for an apprenticeship program, check this list.

Culinary Scoop

What does a julienne carrot look like? A *julienne* carrot is one that has been cut into small, thin strips about two inches long. Chefs often serve julienne vegetables in their restaurants.

DIRECTORY OF CULINARY ARTS TRAINING PROGRAMS

ALABAMA
Bishop State Community College
414 Stanton St.
Mobile 36617
334-473-8692; FAX: 334-471-5961

James H. Faulkner State Community College
3301 Gulf Shores Parkway
Gulf Shores 36542
334-968-3104; FAX: 334-968-3120

Jefferson State Community College
2601 Carson Rd.
Birmingham 35215-3098
205-856-7898; FAX: 205-853-0340
http://www.jscc.cc.al.us/

Lawson State Community College
3060 Wilson Rd. Southwest
Birmingham 35221-1798
205-929-6378; FAX: 205-929-6316

Wallace State Community College
P.O. Box 2000
Hanceville 35077-2000
201-352-8227; FAX: 201-352-8228

ALASKA
University of Alaska, Fairbanks
510 Second Ave.
Fairbanks 99701
907-474-5196; FAX: 907-474-7335

ARIZONA
Arizona Western College
P.O. Box 929
Yuma 85366-0929
520-344-7779; FAX: 520-344-7730

The Art Institute of Phoenix
2233 West Dunlap Ave.
Phoenix 85021-2859
602-678-4300; FAX: 602-216-0439
http://www.aii.edu

Maricopa Skills Centers
1245 East Buckeye Rd.
Phoenix 85034-4101
602-238-4300; FAX: 602-238-4307
http:/www.gwc.maricopa.edu/msc/

Pima Community College
4905 East Broadway
Tucson 85709-1010
520-748-4640; FAX: 520-884-6728

Scottsdale Community College
9000 East Chaparral Rd.
Scottsdale 85250-2699
602-423-6244; FAX: 602-423-6200

Scottsdale Culinary Institute
8100 East Camelback Rd.
Scottsdale 85251
800-848-2433; FAX: 602-990-0351
http://www.chefs.com/culinary

ARKANSAS
Ozarka Technical College
P.O. Box 10
Melbourne 72556
870-368-7371; FAX: 870-368-4733
http://www.ozarka.tec.ar.us

CALIFORNIA
American River College
4700 College Oak Dr.
Sacramento 95841-4286
916-484-8171

Bakersfield College
1801 Panorama Dr.
Bakersfield 93305-1299
805-395-4301; FAX: 805-395-4230
http://www.kccd.cc.ca.us/

Beringer Vineyard's School for American Chefs
2000 Main St.
St. Helena 94574
707-963-7115; FAX: 707-963-2385

Cabrillo College
6500 Soquel Dr.
Aptos 95003-3194
408-479-5749; FAX: 408-479-5769

California Culinary Academy
625 Polk St.
San Francisco 94102
800-BAY-CHEF; FAX: 415-771-2194
http://www.baychef.com

Century Business College
2665 Fifth Ave., Room 115
San Diego 92103
619-233-0184; FAX: 619-233-1302

Cerritos College
1110 Alondra Boulevard
Norwalk 90650
213-860-2451

Chaffey College
5885 Haven Ave.
Rancho Cucamonga 91737-3002
909-941-2711; FAX: 909-466-2831

City College of San Francisco
50 Phelan Ave.
San Francisco 94112-1821
415-239-3908; FAX: 415-239-3913

College of the Desert
43-500 Monterey Ave.
Palm Desert 92260-9305
760-346-8041; FAX: 760-341-8678

College of the Sequoias
915 South Mooney Boulevard
Visalia 93277-2234
209-730-3727; FAX: 209-730-3894

Columbia College
11600 Columbia College Dr.
Sonora 95370
209-588-5231; FAX: 209-588-5104

Columbia School of Culinary Arts
P. O. Box 330
Columbia 95310
209-533-2342; FAX: 209-533-2417

Contra Costa College
2600 Mission Bell Dr.
San Pablo 94806-3195
510-235-7800; FAX: 510-236-6768

The Culinary Institute of America
2555 Main St.
St. Helena 94574
800-333-9242; FAX: 707-967-2410

Cypress College
9200 Valley View St.
Cypress 90630-5897
714-826-2220; FAX: 714-527-1077

Diablo Valley College
321 Golf Club Rd.
Pleasant Hill 94523-1544
510-685-1230; FAX: 510-825-8412

El Camino College
16007 Crenshaw Boulevard
Torrance 90506-0001
310-660-3418

Epicurean School of Culinary Arts
8759 Melrose Ave.
Los Angeles 90069
310-659-5990; FAX: 310-659-0302

Glendale Community College
1500 North Verdugo Rd.
Glendale 91208-2894
818-240-1000; FAX: 818-549-9436

Grossmont College
8800 Grossmont College Dr.
El Cajon 92020-1799
619-644-7327; FAX: 619-461-3396

Laney College
900 Fallon St.
Oakland 94607-4893
510-464-3407; FAX: 510-464-3240

Long Beach City College
4901 East Carson St.
Long Beach 90808-1780
310-938-4130

Los Angeles Culinary Institute
17815 Ventura Boulevard
Encino 91316
888-343-5224

Los Angeles Mission College
13356 Eldridge Ave.
Sylmar 91342-3200
818-364-7658
http://www.lamission.cc.ca.us

Los Angeles Trade-Technical College
400 West Washington Boulevard
Los Angeles 90015-4108
213-744-9480; FAX: 213-748-7334

Mission College
3000 Mission College Boulevard
Santa Clara 95054-1897
408-748-2753; FAX: 408-496-0462
http://www.wvmccd.cc.ca.us/mc

Napa Valley College
1088 College Ave.
St. Helena 94574
707-967-2930; FAX: 707-967-2909

Opportunities Industrialization
Center-West
2050 Broadway
Redwood City 94063
650-568-2883; FAX: 650-568-2884

Orange Coast College
2701 Fairview Rd., P.O. Box 5005
Costa Mesa 92628-5005
714-432-5835

Oxnard College
4000 South Rose Ave.
Oxnard 93033-6699
805-986-5869; FAX: 805-986-5865

Richardson Researches, Inc.
23449 Foley St.
Hayward 94545
510-785-1350; FAX: 510-785-6857
http://www.richres.com

San Joaquin Delta College
5151 Pacific Ave.
Stockton 95207-6370
209-954-5516; FAX: 209-954-5600
http://www.sjccd.cc.ca.us/FCHS/sjdc.html

Santa Barbara City College
721 Cliff Dr.
Santa Barbara 93109-2394
805-965-0851; FAX: 805-963-7222
http://www.fbcc.cc.ca.us/

Santa Rosa Junior College
1501 Mendocino Ave.
Santa Rosa 95401-4395
707-527-4591; FAX: 707-527-4816
http://www.santarosa.edu/

Shasta College
P.O. Box 496006
Redding 96049-6006
916-225-4829; FAX: 916-225-4706

Southern California School of Culinary Arts
1420 El Centro
South Pasadena 91030
888-900-CHEF; FAX: 818-403-8494
E-mail: scsca@earthlink.net

Tanta Marie's Cooking School
271 Francisco St.
San Francisco 94133
415-788-6699; FAX: 415-788-8924

UCLA Extension, Hospitality/
Foodservice Management
10995 Le Conte Ave., Room 515
Los Angeles 90024-0901
310-206-1578; FAX: 310-206-7249

Westlake Culinary Institute
4643 Lakeview Canyon Rd.
Westlake Village 91361
818-991-3940; FAX: 805-495-2554

COLORADO
Colorado Institute of Art
200 East Ninth Ave.
Denver 80203-2983
800-275-2420; FAX: 303-860-8520
http://www.aii.edu

Colorado Mountain College
P.O. Box 10001
Glenwood Springs 81602
800-621-8559; FAX: 970-945-7279
http://www.colordomtn.edu/

Cooking School of the Rockies
637 South Broadway, Ste. H
Boulder 80303
303-494-7988; FAX: 303-494-7999

Culinary Institute of Colorado Springs
5675 South Academy Boulevard
Colorado Springs 80906
719-540-7371; FAX: 719-540-7453
http://www.ppcc.ccoes.edu

Johnson & Wales University at Vail
616 West Lionshead Circle
Vail 81657
970-476-2996; FAX: 970-476-2994
http://www.jwu.edu

Pikes Peak Community College
5675 South Academy Boulevard
Colorado Springs 80906
719-540-7371; FAX: 719-540-7453

Pueblo Community College
900 West Orman Ave.
Pueblo 81004-1499
719-549-3071; FAX: 719-549-3070

School of Natural Cookery
P.O. Box 19466
Boulder 80308
303-444-8068

Warren Tech
13300 West 2nd Place
Lakewood 80228-1256
303-982-8555; FAX: 303-982-8547

CONNECTICUT
Connecticut Culinary Institute
230 Farmington Ave.
Farmington 06032
860-677-7869; FAX: 860-676-0679

Emmett O'Brien Regional Vocational-
Technical School
141 Prindle Ave.
Ansonia 06401
203-732-1800; FAX: 203-735-6236

Gateway Community Technical College
60 Sargent Dr.
New Haven 06511-5918
203-789-7067; FAX: 203-789-6510

Manchester Community-Technical College
P.O. Box 1046
Manchester 06045-1046
860-647-6136; FAX: 860-647-6238

Naugatuck Valley Community-
Technical College
750 Chase Parkway
Waterbury 06708-3000
203-575-8175; FAX: 203-596-8766
http://www.nvctc.commnet.edu/

Norwalk Community-Technical College
188 Richards Ave.
Norwalk 06854-1655
203-857-7355; FAX: 203-857-3327

The Silo Cooking School
Upland Rd.
New Milford 06776
203-355-0300

DELAWARE
Delaware Technical and Community College
400 Stanton-Christiana Rd.
Newark 19713
302-454-3954; FAX: 302-453-3029

FLORIDA
The Academy/American Culinary Arts Program
3131 Flightline Dr.
Lakeland 33811
800-532-3210; FAX: 941-648-2204

The Art Institute of Fort Lauderdale
1799 Southeast 17th St. Causeway
Fort Lauderdale 33316-3000
800-275-7603; FAX: 954-523-7676
http://www.aii.edu

Atlantic Vocational Technical Center
4700 Coconut Creek Parkway
Coconut Creek 33066
305-977-2066

Brevard Community College
1519 Clearlake Rd.
Cocoa 32922-6597
407-632-1111; FAX: 407-633-4565

Charlotte Vocational Technical Center
18300 Toledo Blade Boulevard
Port Charlotte 33948-3399
941-629-6819; FAX: 941-629-2058

Daytona Beach Community College
P.O. Box 2811
Daytona Beach 32120
904-255-8131; FAX: 904-254-3063

Erwin Technical Center
2010 East Hillsborough
Tampa 33610
813-231-1815; FAX: 813-231-1820

Florida Community College at Jacksonville
4501 Capper Rd.
Jacksonville 32218
904-766-6652; FAX: 904-766-6654
http://www.fccj.cc.fl.us/

Florida Culinary Institute
1126 53rd Court
West Palm Beach 33407
561-842-8324; FAX: 561-842-9503
http://www.floridaculinary.com

Fred K. Marchman Vocational-
Technical Center
7825 Campus Dr.
New Port Richey 34653-1211
813-842-7177; FAX: 813-836-3448

Gulf Coast Community College
5230 West Highway 98
Panama City 32401-1058
850-872-3850; FAX: 850-872-3836

Indian River Community College
Fort Pierce 34981-5599
407-462-4740

Johnson & Wales University
1701 Northeast 127th St.
North Miami 33181
800-BEA-CHEF; Fax: 305-892-7020
http://www.jwu.edu

Lake Country Area Vocational-Technical Center
2001 Kurt St.
Eustis 32726
904-357-8222

Lindsey Hopkins Technical
Education Center
750 Northwest 20th St.
Miami 33127
305-324-6070; FAX: 305-545-6397

Lively Area Vocational-Technical Institute
500 Appleyard Dr.
Tallahassee 32304
904-487-7555; FAX: 904-922-3880

Manatee Technical Institute
5603 34th St. West
Bradenton 34210
941-751-7917; FAX: 941-751-7927

McFatter Vocational Technical Center
6500 Nova Dr.
Davie 33317
954-370-8324; FAX: 954-370-1647
http://www.gate.net/~mcfatter

Miami Job Corps Center,
Res-Care, Inc.
660 Southwest Third St.
Miami 33130
305-325-1287

Miami Lakes Technical Education Center
5780 Northwest 158th St.
Miami Lakes 33014
305-557-1100; FAX: 305-557-7391

Mid-Florida Technical Institute
2900 West Oakridge Rd.
Orlando 32809
407-855-5880; FAX: 407-855-5880

North Technical Education Center
7071 Garden Rd.
Riviera Beach 33404
561-881-4600; FAX: 561-881-4668

Pensacola Junior College
1000 College Boulevard
Pensacola 32504-8998
850-484-1422; FAX: 850-484-1543

Pinellas Technical Education Center-
Clearwater Campus
6100 154th Ave. North
Clearwater 33760
813-538-7167; FAX: 813-538-7203

Pinellas Technical Educational Center
901 34th St. South
St. Petersburg 33711
813-327-3671

Robert Morgan Vocational Technical Center
18180 Southwest 122nd Ave.
Miami 33177
305-253-9920; FAX: 305-253-3023

Sarasota County Technical Institute
4748 Beneva Rd.
Sarasota 34233
941-924-1365

Schwettman Adult Education
5520 Grand Boulevard
New Port Richey 34652
813-842-5714

Seminole Community College
Sanford 32773
407-328-2186; FAX: 407-328-2186

South Florida Community College
600 West College Dr.
Avon Park 33825
941-382-6900; FAX: 941-453-2365

South Technical Education Center
1300 Southwest 30th Ave.
Boynton Beach 33426
561-369-7000; FAX: 561-369-7024

The Southeast Institute of the Culinary Arts
2980 Collins Ave.
St. Augustine 32095
904-829-1061; FAX: 904-824-6750

Southeastern Academy
P.O. Box 421768
Kissimmee 34742-1768
407-847-4444; FAX: 407-847-8793

Washington Holmes Area
Vocational-Technical
209 Hoyt St.
Chipley 32428
904-357-8222

GEORGIA
Albany Technical Institute
1021 Lowe Rd.
Albany 31708
912-430-3500

The Art Institute of Atlanta
3376 Peachtree Rd. Northeast
Atlanta 30326-1018
404-266-1383; FAX: 404-898-9551
http://www.aii.edu

Atlanta Technical Institute
1560 Metropolitan Parkway
Atlanta 30310
404-756-3727; FAX: 404-756-0932

Augusta Technical Institute
3116 Deans Bridge Rd.
Augusta 30906
706-771-4083; FAX: 706-771-4016

Ben Hill-Irwin Technical Institute
P.O. Box 1069
Fitzgerald 31750
912-468-7487

Middle Georgia Technical Institute
1311 Corder Rd.
Warner Robins 31088
912-929-6800; FAX: 912-929-6835

Savannah Technical Institute
5717 White Bluff Rd.
Savannah 31499
912-351-4553; FAX: 912-351-4526

HAWAII
University of Hawaii-
Kapiolani Community College
4303 Diamond Head Rd.
Honolulu 96816-4421
808-734-9466; FAX: 808-734-9212

University of Hawaii-
Kauai Community College
3-1901 Kaumualii Highway
Lihue 96766-9591
808-245-8225; FAX: 808-245-8297

University of Hawaii-
Maui Community College
310 Kaahumanu Ave.
Kahului 96732
808-984-3225; FAX: 808-984-3314

IDAHO
Boise State University
1910 University Dr.
Boise 83725-0399
208-385-1431

College of Southern Idaho
Twin Falls 83303-1238
208-733-9554; FAX: 208-736-3014

Idaho State University
Box 8380
Pocatello 83209
208-236-3327; FAX: 208-236-4641

North Idaho College
Coeur d'Alene 83814-2199
208-769-3311; FAX: 208-769-3431
http://www.nidc.edu/

ILLINOIS
Belleville Area College
4950 Maryville Rd.
Granite City 62040
618-931-0600

Black Hawk College
6600 34th Ave.
Moline 61265-5899
309-796-1311; FAX: 309-792-3418

College of DuPage
425 22nd St.
Glen Ellyn 60137
630-942-2315; FAX: 630-858-9399

College of Lake County
19351 West Washington St.
Grayslake 60030-1198
847-343-2823; FAX: 847-223-7248

Cooking Academy of Chicago
2500 West Bradley Place
Chicago 60618
773-478-9840; FAX: 773-478-3146

The Cooking and Hospitality Institute of Chicago
361 West Chestnut St.
Chicago 60610-3050
312-944-0882; FAX: 312-944-8557
http://www.chicnet.org

Elgin Community College
1700 Spartan Dr.
Elgin 60123-7193
847-697-1000; FAX: 847-931-3911
http://www.elgin.cc.il.us

Joliet Junior College
1216 Houbolt Ave.
Joliet 60436
815-729-9020

Kendall College
2408 Orrington Ave.
Evanston 60201-2899
847-866-1300; FAX: 847-866-1320

Lexington College
10840 South Western Ave.
Chicago 60643-3294
773-779-3800; FAX: 773-779-7450

Lincoln Land Community College
Shepherd Rd.
Springfield 62794-9256
217-786-2772; FAX: 217-786-2495

Moraine Valley Community College
10900 South 88th Ave.
Palos Hills 60465-0937
708-974-5320; FAX: 708-974-1184
http://www.moraine.cc.il.us

Rend Lake College
Ina 62846-9801
618-437-5321
http://www.rlc.cc.il.us/

Triton College
2000 5th Ave.
River Grove 60171-9983
708-456-0300; FAX: 708-583-3108

Washburne Trade School
3233 West 31st St.
Chicago 60623
773-579-6100; FAX: 773-376-5940

William Rainey Harper College
1200 West Algonquin Rd.
Palatine 60067-7398
847-925-6206; FAX: 847-925-6044
http://www.harper.cc.il.us

Wilton School of Cake Decorating
2240 West 75th St.
Woodbridge 60517
630-963-7100; FAX: 630-963-7299

INDIANA
Ball State University
2000 University Ave.
Muncie 47306-1099
765-285-5931; FAX: 765-285-2314

Indiana University-Purdue
University Fort Wayne
Neff Hall, Room 330B
Fort Wayne 46805-1499
219-481-6562; FAX: 219-481-5472

Ivy Tech State College-Central Indiana
One West 26th St., P.O. Box 1763
Indianapolis 46206-1763
317-921-4619; Fax: 317-921-4753

Ivy Tech State College-Northwest
1440 East 35th Ave.
Gary 46409-1499
219-981-4400; Fax: 219-981-4415

Vincennes University
1002 North First St.
Vincennes 47591-5202
812-888-4313; FAX: 812-888-5868

IOWA
Clinton Community College
Clinton 52732-6299
319-242-6841

Des Moines Area Community College
2006 South Ankeny Boulevard,
Bldg. #7
Ankeny 50021-8995
515-964-6532; FAX: 515-964-6486

Eastern Iowa Community College District
306 West River Dr.
Davenport 52801
319-322-5015; FAX: 319-322-3956

Indian Hills Community College
525 Grandview
Ottumwa 52501
515-683-5195; FAX: 515-683-5184

Iowa Lakes Community College
3200 College Dr.
Emmetsburg 50536-1098
712-852-5256; FAX: 712-852-2152

Iowa Western Community College
Council Bluffs 51502
712-325-3288; FAX: 712-325-3720

Kirkwood Community College
6301 Kirkwood Boulevard Southwest
Cedar Rapids 52406
319-398-4981; FAX: 319-398-5667
http://www.kirkwood.cc.ia.us/

Scott Community College
500 Belmont Rd.
Bettendorf 52722-6804
319-359-7531

KANSAS

American Institute of Baking
1213 Bakers Way
Manhattan 66502
800-633-5137; FAX: 785-537-1493
http://www.aibonline.org

Flint Hills Technical School
3301 West 18th Ave.
Emporia 66801
316-341-2300; FAX: 316-343-7252

Johnson County Community College
12345 College at Quivira
Overland Park 66210-1299
913-469-8500
http://www.johnco.cc.ks.us/

Kansas City Kansas Area
Vocational Technical School
2220 North 59th St.
Kansas City 66104
913-596-5500; FAX: 913-596-5509

Northeast Kansas Area Vocational
Technical School
1501 West Riley
Atchison 66002
913-367-6204; FAX: 913-367-3107

Wichita Area Technical College
324 North Emporia
Wichita 67217
316-833-4360; FAX: 316-833-4341

KENTUCKY

Earle C. Clements Job Corps Center
P.O. Box 5000
U.S. Highway 60
Morganfield 42437
502-389-2419; FAX: 502-389-1134

Kentucky Tech Elizabethtown
505 University Dr.
Elizabethtown 42701
502-766-5133; FAX: 502-737-0505

Kentucky Tech-Davies County Campus
15th and Frederica St.
Owensboro 42301
502-687-7260; FAX: 502-687-7208

Kentucky Tech-Jefferson Campus
727 West Chestnut St.
Louisville 40203
502-595-4136; FAX: 502-595-4399

Sullivan College
3101 Bardstown Rd.
Louisville 40205
800-844-1354; FAX: 502-454-4880

University of Kentucky,
Jefferson Community College
109 East Broadway
Louisville 40202-2005
502-584-0181; FAX: 502-584-0181

West Kentucky State Vocational
Technical School
Blandville Rd., Box 7408
Paducah 42002
502-554-4991; FAX: 502-554-9754

LOUISIANA

Bossier-Parish Community College
2719 Airline Dr. North
Bossier City 71111
318-746-6120

Culinary Arts Institute of Louisiana
427 Lafayette St.
Baton Rouge 70802
504-343-6233; FAX: 504-338-4880

Delgado Community College
615 City Park Ave.
New Orleans 70119-4399
504-483-4208; FAX: 504-483-4893
http:/www.dcc.edu/

Elaine P. Nunez Community College
3700 LaFontaine St.
Chalmette 70043-1249
504-278-7350; FAX: 504-278-7353
http://www.nunez.cc.la.us

Louisiana Technical College-
Baton Rouge Campus
3250 North Acadian Highway E
Baton Rouge LA 70805
504-359-9226; FAX: 504-359-9296

Louisiana Technical College-
Lafayette Campus
1101 Bertrand Dr.
Lafayette 70506
318-262-5962; FAX: 318-262-5122

Louisiana Technical College-New Orleans
9800 Navarre Ave.
New Orleans 70124
504-483-4626; FAX: 504-483-4643

Louisiana Technical College-
Sidney N. Collier Campus
3727 Louisa St.
New Orleans 70126
504-942-8333; FAX: 504-942-8337

Louisiana Technical College-
Sowela Campus
3820 J. Bennett Johnston Ave.
Lake Charles 70615
318-491-2687; FAX: 318-491-2135

Nicolls State University
P.O. Box 2099
Thibodaux 70310
504-449-7100; FAX: 504-449-7089

Sclafani's Cooking School, Inc.
107 Gennaro Place
Metairie 70001
800-583-1282; FAX: 504-833-7872
http://www.gnofn.org/~sclafani

MAINE
Southern Maine Technical College
Fort Rd.
South Portland 04106
207-767-9520; FAX: 207-767-9671

York County Technical College
Wells 04090
207-646-9282; FAX: 207-641-0837

MARYLAND
Baltimore International College
17 Commerce St.
Baltimore 21202-3230
410-752-4710; FAX: 410-752-3730
http://www.bicc.edu

Chesapeake Institute of Culinary Studies
Route 249
Piney Point 20674
301-994-0010; FAX: 301-994-2180

International School of Confectionery
Arts, Inc.
9209 Gaither Rd.
Gaithersburg 20877
301-963-9077; FAX: 301-869-7669

L'Academie de Cuisine
16006 Industrial Dr.
Gaithersburg MD 20877
301-670-8670; FAX: 301-670-0450
http://www.lacademie.com

MASSACHUSETTS
Bay Path Regional Vocational-Technical
57 Old Muggett Hill Rd.
Charlton 01507-1331
508-987-1078

Berkshire Community College
1350 West St.
Pittsfield 01201-5786
413-499-4660; FAX: 413-447-7840
http://www.cbcc.bcwan.net/

Blue Hills Regional Technical School
800 Randolph St.
Canton 02021
617-828-5800; FAX: 617-828-0794

Boston University Culinary Arts
808 Commonwealth Ave.
Boston 02215
617-353-9852; FAX: 617-353-4130

Bristol Community College
777 Elsbree St.
Fall River 02720-7395
508-678-2811; FAX: 508-676-7146

Bunker Hill Community College
250 New Rutherford Ave.
Boston 02129
617-228-2417; FAX: 617-228-2082

The Cambridge School of Culinary Arts
2020 Massachusetts Ave.
Cambridge 02140-2124
617-354-2020; FAX: 617-576-1963

Endicott College
376 Hale St.
Beverly 01915-2096
800-325-1114; FAX: 978-232-2520
http://www.endicott.edu

Essex Agricultural and Technical Institute
562 Maple St.
P.O. Box 562
Hathorne 01937
508-774-0050; FAX: 508-774-6530

Holyoke Community College
303 Homestead Ave.
Holyoke 01040-1099
413-552-2229; FAX: 413-534-8975
http://www.hcc.mass.edu/

Massasoit Community College
One Massasoit Boulevard
Brockton 02402-3996
508-588-9100

Minuteman Regional Vocational
Technical School
758 Marrett Rd.
Lexington 02173
614-861-6500; FAX: 617-863-1254

Newbury College
129 Fisher Ave.
Brookline 02146-5750
617-730-7007; FAX: 617-731-9618
http://www.newbury.edu

MICHIGAN
Charles Stewart Mott Community College
1401 East Court St.
Flint 48503-2089
810-232-7845; FAX: 810-232-9442
http://www.mcc.edu/

Culinary Arts Studio
2418 Eleven Mile Rd.
Madison Heights 48071
810-541-0806; FAX: 810-547-1009

Grand Rapids Community College
151 Fountain St. Northeast
Grand Rapids 49503
616-771-3690; FAX: 616-771-3698
http://www.grcc.cc.mi.us/hed

Henry Ford Community College
5101 Evergreen Rd.
Dearborn 48128-1495
313-845-6390; FAX: 313-845-9784
http://www.henryford.cc.mi.us/

Macomb Community College
44575 Garfield Rd., K-124-1
Clinton Township 48316
810-286-2088; FAX: 810-286-2038

Monroe County Community College
1555 South Raisinville Rd.
Monroe 48161-9047
313-384-4150; FAX: 313-242-9711

Northern Michigan University
1401 Presque Isle Ave.
Marquette 49855-5301
906-227-2066; FAX: 906-227-1549

Northwestern Michigan College
1701 East Front St.
Traverse City 49686-3061
616-922-1197; FAX: 616-922-1134
http://www.nmc.edu/

Oakland Community College
27055 Orchard Lake Rd.
Farmington Hills 48334
248-471-7786; FAX: 248-471-7553
http://www.occ.cc.mi.us/

Schoolcraft College
18600 Haggerty Rd.
Livonia 48152-2696
313-462-4423; FAX: 313-462-4581
http://www.schoolcraft.cc.mi.us

Washtenaw Community College
4800 East Huron River Dr.
P.O. Box D-1
Ann Arbor 48106
313-973-3601; FAX: 313-677-5414

Wayne County Community College
801 West Fort St.
Detroit 48226-9975
313-496-2539; FAX: 313-961-2791

MINNESOTA
Alexandria Technical College
1601 Jefferson St.
Alexandria 56308-3707
320-762-0221; FAX: 320-762-4501
http://www.atc.tec.mn.us/

Duluth Technical College
2101 Trinity Rd.
Duluth 55811
218-722-2801

Hennepin Technical College
9000 Brooklyn Boulevard
Brooklyn Park 55445
612-425-3800; FAX: 612-550-2119

Hibbing Community College
2900 East Beltline, Central Bldg.
Hibbing 55746-3300
218-262-6716
http://www.hibbing.tec.mn.us

Minneapolis Community Technical College
1501 Hennepin Ave. South
Minneapolis 55403
612-341-7040

National Baking Center
818 Dunwoody Boulevard
Minneapolis 55403
612-374-3303; FAX: 612-374-3332
http://www.dunwoody.tec.mn.us/nbc.htm

Northwest Technical College
1900 28th Ave. South
Moorhead 56560
218-299-6512; FAX: 218-236-0342
http://www.ntc-online.com

St. Cloud Technical College
1540 Northway Dr.
St. Cloud 56303-1240
320-654-5089; FAX: 320-654-5981
http://www.stcloud.mn.us.edu/sctc

St. Paul Technical College
235 Marshall Ave.
St. Paul 55102
612-221-1300; FAX: 612-221-1416
http://www.sptc.tec.mn.us

South Central Technical College
1920 Lee Boulevard
North Mankato 56003
507-389-7229; FAX: 507-388-9951

MISSISSIPPI
Mississippi University for Women
Culinary Arts Institute
Box W1639
Columbus 39701
601-241-7472; FAX: 601-241-7627
http://www.muw.edu/interdisc

Offshore Cooking School
703 Cox Ave.
Ocean Springs 39564
601-875-1333; FAX: 601-392-0209

MISSOURI
Missouri Culinary Institute
13 & 24 Highway Junction
Route 1, Box 224F
Lexington 64067
816-259-6464

Penn Valley Community College
3201 Southwest Trafficway
Kansas City 64111
816-759-4101

St. Louis Community College at Forest Park
560 Oakland Ave.
St. Louis 63110-1316
314-644-9767; FAX: 314-951-9405

MONTANA
Montana State University
1500 North 30th St.
Billings 59101
406-657-2158; FAX: 406-657-2302

Montana State University of Technology-Great Falls
2100 16th Ave. South
Great Falls 59405
406-771-4310; FAX: 406-771-4317

The University of Montana Missoula
909 South Ave. West
Missoula 59801
406-243-7811; FAX: 406-243-7899

NEBRASKA
Central Community College-Hastings Campus
P.O. Box 1024
Hastings 68902-1024
402-463-9811; FAX: 402-461-2454

Metropolitan Community College
P.O. Box 3777
Omaha 68103-0777
402-457-2510; FAX: 402-457-2515
http://www.mcc.neb.edu

Southeast Community College, Lincoln Campus
8800 O St.
Lincoln 68520-1299
402-437-2465; FAX: 402-437-2404

NEVADA
Community College of Southern Nevada
3200 East Cheyene
North Las Vegas 89030
702-651-4192; FAX: 702-651-4743

Southern Nevada Vocational
Technical Center
5710 Mt. Vista
Las Vegas 89120
702-451-1088

Truckee Meadows Community College
7000 Dandini Boulevard
Reno 89512-3901
702-673-7096; FAX: 702-673-7018

University of Nevada, Las Vegas
4505 Maryland Parkway
Las Vegas 89154-1021
702-895-3443; FAX: 702-895-1118
http://www.unlv.edu

NEW HAMPSHIRE
New Hampshire College
2500 North River Rd.
Manchester 03106-1045
800-642-4968; FAX: 603-645-9693
http://www.nhc.edu

New Hampshire Community College
Technical College
2020 Riverside Dr.
Berlin 03570-3717
603-752-1113; FAX: 603-752-6335

University of New Hampshire
Cole Hall, Mast Rd.
Durham 03824
603-862-1025; FAX: 603-862-2915

NEW JERSEY
Atlantic Community College
5100 Black Horse Pike
Mays Landing 08330-2699
609-343-5009; FAX: 609-343-4921
http://www.atlantic.edu/

Bergen Community College
400 Paramus Rd.
Paramus 07652-1595
201-447-7192; FAX: 201-612-5240

Burlington County College
Route 530
Pemberton 08068-1599
609-894-9311; FAX: 609-726-0442
http://www.bcc.edu/

Hudson County Community College
161 Newkirk St.
Jersey City 07306
201-714-2193; FAX: 201-656-1522
http://www.hudson.cc.nj.us/

Middlesex County College
2600 Woodbridge Ave.
P.O. Box 3050
Edison 08818-3050
732-906-2538; FAX: 732-561-1885
http://www.njin.net/mcc/

Morris County School of Technology
400 East Main St.
Denville 07834
201-627-4600; FAX: 201-627-6979

Passaic County Technical Institute
45 Reinhardt Rd.
Wayne 07470
201-389-4296

Salem County Vocational Technical Schools
P.O. Box 350
Woodstown 08098
609-769-0101; FAX: 609-769-4214

NEW MEXICO
Albuquerque Culinary Arts Center
9317 Guadalupe Trail Northwest
Alameda 87114
505-898-1640

Albuquerque Technical Vocational Institute
525 Buena Vista Southeast
Albuquerque 87106-4096
505-224-3210
http://www.tvi.cc.nm.us/

Crownpoint Institute of Technology
P.O. Box 849, Chaco Rd.
Crownpoint 87313
505-786-5851; FAX: 505-786-5644

Luna Vocational Technical Institute
P.O. Drawer K
Las Vegas 87701
505-454-1484

San Juan College
4601 College Boulevard
Farmington 87401
505-326-3311

Santa Fe Community College
P.O. Box 4187
6401 Richards Ave.
Santa Fe 87502-4187
505-438-1600; FAX: 505-438-1237

Southwestern Indian Polytechnic Institute
9169 Coors Northwest, Box 10146
Albuquerque 87184-0146
505-897-5359; FAX: 505-897-5343

Technical Vocational Institute Community College
900 University Boulevard Southeast
Albuquerque 87106
505-224-3194

NEW YORK
Adirondack Community College
640 Bay Rd.
Queensbury 12804
518-743-2200; FAX: 518-743-2264

Cattaraugus Allegany County
BOCES Center at Ellicottville
Route 242, Box 690
Ellicottville 14731-0690
716-699-2382; FAX: 716-699-2095

Culinary Institute of America
433 Albany Post Rd.
Hyde Park 12538-1499
800-CULINARY
http://www.ciachef.edu

Erie Community College, City Campus
121 Ellicott St.
Buffalo 14203-2601
716-851-1035; FAX: 716-851-1129
http://www.sunyerie.davey.edu/

The French Culinary Institute
462 Broadway
New York 10013
888-FCI-CHEF; FAX: 212-431-3054
http://www.frenchculinary.com

Jefferson Community College
Outer Coffeen St.
Watertown 13601
315-786-2277; FAX: 315-786-2459
http://www.sunyjefferson.edu/

Julie Sahni's School of Indian Cooking
101 Clark St.
Brooklyn 11201-2746
718-625-3958; FAX: 718-625-3456

Mohawk Valley Community College
1101 Sherman Dr.
Utica 13501-5394
315-792-5354; FAX: 315-792-5527
http://www.mvcc.edu/

Monroe Community College
1000 East Henrietta Rd.
Rochester 14623-5780
716-292-2586; FAX: 716-427-2749
http://www.monroecc.edu/

Natural Gourmet Cooking School
48 West 21st St., 2nd fl.
New York 10010
212-645-5170; FAX: 212-989-1493

New School for Social Research
100 Greenwich Ave.
New York 10011-8603
212-255-4141; FAX: 212-807-0406

New York City Technical College
300 Jay St. #N220
Brooklyn 11201
718-260-5630; FAX: 718-260-5997

New York Food and Hotel Management School
154 West 14th St.
New York 10011
212-675-6655; FAX: 212-463-9194

New York Institute of Technology
Culinary Arts Center
300 Carleton Ave. #66-101
Central Islip 11722-9029
516-348-3310; FAX: 516-348-3247
http://www.nyit.edu/culinary

New York Restaurant School
75 Varick St., 16th fl.
New York 10013
212-226-5500; FAX: 212-226-5644
http://www.aii.edu

New York University
35 West 4th St., 10th fl.
New York 10012-1172
212-998-5591; FAX: 212-995-4194
http://www.nyu.edu/education/nutrition/

Niagara County Community College
3111 South Saunders Settlement Rd.
Sanborn 14132-9460
716-731-3271; FAX: 716-731-4053
http://www.sunyniagara.cc.ny.us

Onondaga Community College
4941 Onondaga Rd.
Syracuse 13215
315-469-2231; FAX: 315-464-6775
http://www.sunyocc.edu/

Paul Smith's College of Arts and Sciences
Routes 86 and 30, P.O. Box 265
Paul Smiths 12970
518-327-6227; FAX: 518-327-6161
http://www.paulsmiths.edu/

Peter Kump's New York Cooking School
307 East 92nd St.
New York 10128
800-522-4610; FAX: 212-348-6360
http://www.pkcookschool.com

Schenectady County Community College
78 Washington Ave.
Schenectady 12305-2294
518-381-1370; FAX: 518-346-0379

State University of New York College of
Agriculture and Technology at Cobleskill
Cobleskill 12043
518-234-5425; FAX: 518-234-5333
http://www.cobleskill.edu/

State University of New York College of
Technology at Alfred
Upper College Dr.
Alfred 14802
607-587-4215
http://www.alfredtech.edu/

State University of New York College of
Technology at Delhi
Main St.
Delhi 13753
607-746-4550; FAX: 607-746-4104
http://www.delhi.edu/

Sullivan County Community College
P.O. Box 4002
Loch Sheldrake 12759-4002
800-577-5243; FAX: 914-434-4806

Syracuse University
034 Slocum Hall
Syracuse 13244
315-443-2386; FAX: 315-443-2562

Westchester Community College
75 Grasslands Rd.
Valhalla 10595-1698
914-785-6551; FAX: 914-785-6423

NORTH CAROLINA
Ashville-Buncombe Technical Community College
340 Victoria Rd.
Asheville 28801-4897
704-254-1921; FAX: 704-251-6355

Central Piedmont Community College
P.O. Box 35009
Charlotte 28235-5009
704-330-6721; FAX: 704-330-6581
http://www.cpcc.cc.nc.us/

Guilford Technical Community College
P.O. Box 309
Jamestown 27282-0309
910-454-1126; FAX: 910-454-2510
http://www.technet.gtec.cc.nc.us/

Sandhills Community College
2200 Airport Rd.
Pinehurst 28374-8299
910-695-3756; FAX: 910-695-1823
http:/www.sandhills.cc.nc.us

Wake Technical Community College
9101 Fayetteville Rd.
Raleigh 27603-5696
919-662-3400; FAX: 919-779-3360

NORTH DAKOTA
North Dakota State College of Science
800 North Sixth St.
Wahpeton 58076
701-671-2264; FAX: 701-671-2126
http://www.ndscs.edu

OHIO
Ashland County-West Holmes Career Center
1783 State Route 60
Ashland 44805-9377
419-289-3313; FAX: 419-289-3729

Cincinnati State Technical and Community College
3520 Central Parkway
Cincinnati 45223-2690
513-569-1662; FAX: 513-569-1467

The Cleveland Restaurant Cooking School
2801 Bridge Ave.
Cleveland 44113
216-771-7130; FAX: 216-771-8130

Columbus State Community College
P.O. Box 1609
Columbus 43216-1609
614-227-2579; FAX: 614-227-5146

Cuyahoga Community College
2900 Community College Ave.
Cleveland 44115
216-987-4082; FAX: 216-987-4086
http://www.tri-c.cc.oh.us/metro

Cuyahoga Community College, Eastern Campus
4250 Richmond Rd.
Highland Hills 44122-6104
216-987-2019
http://www.tri-cc.oh.us/east/

Hocking College
3301 Hocking Parkway
Nelsonville 45764-9588
614-753-3531; FAX: 614-753-9158
http://www.hocking.cc.oh.us

The Loretta Paganini School of Cooking
8613 Mayfield Rd.
Chesterland 44026
440-729-1110; FAX: 440-729-6459

Owens Community College
P.O. Box 10000, Oregon Rd.
Toledo 43699-1947
419-661-7359; FAX: 419-661-7665

Sinclair Community College
444 West Third St.
Dayton 45402-1460
937-449-5197; FAX: 937-449-4530
http://www.sinclair.edu

University of Akron
102 Gallucci Hall
Akron 44325-7907
330-972-5393; FAX: 330-972-5525

Zona Spray Cooking School
140 North Main
Hudson 44236
216-6950-1665

OKLAHOMA

Great Plains Area Vocational Technical Center
4500 West Lee Boulevard
Lawton 73505
405-250-5622; FAX: 405-250-5677

Meridian Technology Center
1312 South Sangre Rd.
Stillwater 74074
405-377-3333
http://www.meridian-technology.com

Metro Area Vocational Technical School
District 22
1720 Springlake Dr.
Oklahoma City 73111
405-424-8324; FAX: 405-424-9403

Oklahoma State University, Okmulgee
1801 East Fourth St.
Okmulgee 74447-3901
800-772-4471; FAX: 918-756-1315

Pioneer Area Vocational
Technical School
2101 North Ash
Ponca City 74601
405-762-8336; FAX: 405-765-5101

Southern Oklahoma Area Vocational
Technical School
2610 San Noble Parkway
Ardmore 73401
405-223-2070; FAX: 405-226-9389

OREGON

Central Oregon Community College
2600 Northwest College Way
Bend 97701-5998
541-383-7713; FAX: 541-383-7708
http://www.cocc.edu/

International School of Baking
1971 Northwest Juniper Ave.
Bend 97701
541-389-8553; FAX: 541-389-3736
http://www.empnet.com/domocorp/

Lane Community College
4000 East 30th Ave.
Eugene 97405-0640
541-747-4501; FAX: 541-744-3995
http://www.lanecc.edu/

Linn-Benton Community College
6500 Southwest Pacific Boulevard
Albany 97321
541-917-4388; FAX: 541-917-4395

Western Culinary Institute
1316 Southwest 13th Ave.
Portland 97201-3355
800-666-0312; FAX: 503-223-0126
http://www.westernculinary.com

PENNSYLVANIA
American Academy of Independent Studies, Inc.
100 North Main Ave.
Scranton 18504
717-969-1949

The Art Institute of Philadelphia
2300 Market St.
Philadelphia 19103
215-567-7080; FAX: 215-564-0241
http://www.aii.edu

Bucks County Community College
Swamp Rd.
Newtown 18940-1525
215-968-8241
http://www.bucks.edu

Community College of Allegheny County
Allegheny Campus
808 Ridge Ave.
Pittsburgh 15212-6003
412-237-2525; FAX: 412-237-4678
http://www.ccac.edu/

Community College of Allegheny County
Boyce Campus
595 Beatty Rd.
Monroeville 15146
412-371-8651

Community College of Beaver County
One Campus Dr.
Monaca 15061-2588
412-775-8561; FAX: 412-775-4055
http://www.ontv.com/college/ccbc.htm

Community College of Philadelphia
1700 Spring Garden St.
Philadelphia 19130-3991
215-751-8797; FAX: 215-972-6388
http://www.ccp.cc.pa.us

Drexel University
3141 Chestnut St.
Philadelphia 19104-2875
215-895-4919; FAX: 215-895-4917
http://www.drexel.edu

Harrisburg Area Community College
One HACC Dr.
Harrisburg 17110-2999
717-780-2674; FAX: 717-231-7670

Hiram G. Andrews Center
727 Goucher St.
Johnstown 15905
814-255-8372; FAX: 814-255-3406

Indiana University of Pennsylvania
Reschini Bldg.
Indiana 15705
800-727-0997; FAX: 412-357-6200
http://www.iup.edu/cularts

International Culinary Academy
107 Sixth St., Fulton Bldg.
Pittsburgh 15222
412-471-9330; FAX: 412-391-4224
http://www.intlculinary.com

JNA Institute of Culinary Arts
1212 South Broad St.
Philadelphia 19146
215-468-8800; FAX: 215-468-8838
http://www.culinaryarts.com

Keystone College
Harris Hall 204
LaPlume 18440-0200
717-945-45141; FAX: 717-945-6960
http://www.keystone.edu/

Lehigh County Community College
2370 Main St.
Schnecksville 18078
610-799-1134

Luzerne County Community College
Nanticoke 18634-9804
717-740-7336

Mercyhurst College
501 East 38th St.
Erie 16546
800-825-1926; FAX: 814-824-2179

Northampton County Area Community College
3835 Green Pond Rd.
Bethlehem 18017-7599
610-861-5593
http://www.nrhm.cc.pa.us/

Orleans Technical Institute
1330 Rhawn St.
Philadelphia 19111
215-728-4488

Pennsylvania College of Technology
One College Ave.
Williamsport 17701-5778
717-326-3761
http://www.pct.edu

Pennsylvania Institute of Culinary Arts
717 Liberty Ave.
Pittsburgh 15222
800-432-2433; FAX: 412-566-2434
http://www.paculinary.com

Reading Area Community College
P.O. Box 1706
Reading 19603-1706
610-372-4721; FAX: 610-375-8255

The Restaurant School
4207 Walnut St.
Philadelphia 19104-3518
215-222-4200; FAX: 215-222-4219

Westmoreland County Community College
Armbrust Rd.
Youngwood 15697
412-925-4064; FAX: 412-925-1150
http://www.westmoreland.cc.pa.us

RHODE ISLAND
Johnson & Wales University
8 Abbott Park Place
Providence 02903-3703
800-342-5598; FAX: 401-598-1835
http://www.jwu.edu

SOUTH CAROLINA
Greenville Technical College
P.O. Box 5616
Greenville 29606-5616
864-250-8030; FAX: 864-250-8455

Horry-Georgetown Technical College
2050 Highway 501, P.O. Box 1966
Conway 29526
803-347-3186; FAX: 803-347-4207

Johnson & Wales University
PCC Box 1409, 701 East Bay St.
Charleston 29403
803-727-3000; FAX: 803-763-0318
http://www.jwu.edu

Trident Technical College
P.O. Box 118067
Charleston 29423-8067
803-722-5571; FAX: 803-720-5614
http://www.charleston.net/trident.tec

SOUTH DAKOTA
Mitchell Technical Institute
821 North Capital
Mitchell 57301
605-995-3024; FAX: 605-996-3299

TENNESSEE
Memphis Culinary Academy
1252 Peabody Ave.
Memphis 38104
901-722-8892

Nashville State Technical Institute
120 White Bridge Rd.
Nashville 37209-4515
615-353-3214; FAX: 615-353-3243
http://www.nsti.tec.tn.us/

Opryland Hotel Culinary Institute
2800 Opryland Dr.
Nashville 37214
615-871-7765; FAX: 615-871-7872

TEXAS
Aims Academy
7015 Greenville Ave.
Dallas 75231
214-988-3202; FAX: 214-660-6058

The Art Institute of Houston
1900 Yorktown
Houston 77056-4115
800-275-4244; FAX: 713-966-2797
http://www.aii.edu

Del Mar College
101 Baldwin Boulevard
Corpus Christi 78404-3897
512-886-1734; FAX: 512-886-1829

El Centro College
Main and Lamar Streets
Dallas 75202-3604
214-860-2202; FAX: 214-860-2335

El Paso Community College
P.O. Box 20500
El Paso 79998-0500
915-594-2217; FAX: 915-594-2155

Galveston College
4015 Ave. Q
Galveston 77550-7496
409-763-6551; FAX: 409-762-9367

Houston Community College System
1300 Holman
Houston 77004
713-718-6046; FAX: 713-718-6054
http://www.hccs.cc.tx.us/

Le Chef College of Hospitality Careers
6020 Dillard Circle
Austin 78752
888-5LE-CHEF; FAX: 512-323-2126
http://www.lechef.org

Odessa College
201 West University
Odessa 79764-7127
915-335-6320; FAX: 915-335-6860

St. Philip's College
1801 Martin Luther King Dr.
San Antonio 78203-2098
210-531-3315; FAX: 210-531-3351

San Jacinto College
North Campus
5800 Uvalde
Houston 77049-4599
281-458-4050; FAX: 281-459-7132

Texas State Technical College-
Waco/Marshall Campus
3801 Campus Dr.
Waco 76705-1695
254-867-4868; FAX: 254-867-3663
http://www.tsc.edu/waco.html

UTAH
Salt Lake Community College
P.O. Box 30808
Salt Lake City 84130-0808
801-957-4066; FAX: 801-957-4895

Utah Valley State College
800 West 1200 South St.
Orem 84058-0001
801-222-8087; FAX: 801-222-8769

VERMONT
New England Culinary Institute
250 Main St.
Montpelier 05602-9720
802-223-6324; FAX: 802-223-0634
http://www.neculinary.com/

VIRGINIA
ATI-Career Institute-School of Culinary Arts
7777 Leesburg Pike
Falls Church 22043
703-821-8570; FAX: 703-821-9289

J. Sargeant Reynolds Community College
701 East Jackson St.
Richmond 23219
804-786-2069; FAX: 804-786-5465
http://www.jsrcc.va.us/dtcbusdiv/hospitality

Johnson & Wales University
2428 Almeda Ave., Ste. 316-318
Norfolk 23513
757-853-1906; FAX: 757-855-8271
http://www.jwu.edu

Tidewater Community College
Virginia Beach Campus
1700 College Crescent
Virginia Beach 23456
804-427-7133

WASHINGTON
The Art Institute of Seattle
2323 Elliott Ave.
Seattle 98121-1622
800-275-2471; FAX: 206-448-2501
http://www.aii.edu

Bates Technical College
1101 South Yakima Ave.
Tacoma 98405
253-596-1566; FAX: 253-596-1643

Bellingham Technical College
3028 Lindbergh Ave.
Bellingham 98225-1599
360-715-8350; FAX: 360-676-2798

Clark College
1800 East McLoughlin Boulevard
Vancouver 98663-3598
360-992-2143; FAX: 360-992-2861
http://www.clark.edu/

Edmonds Community College
20000 68th Ave. West
Lynnwood 98036-5999
425-640-1329; FAX: 425-771-3366
http://www.edcc.edu/

Kitsop Peninsula Vocational Skills Center
101 National Ave. North
Bremerton 98312
206-478-6083; FAX: 206-478-5090

North Seattle Community College
9600 College Way North
Seattle 98103-3599
206-527-3779; FAX: 206-527-3635
http://www.scc.cc.wa.us/sccd/north/norsea.html

Olympic College
1600 Chester Ave.
Bremerton 98337-1699
360-478-4576; FAX: 360-478-4650
http://www.web.etc.edu/

Renton Technical College
3000 Fourth St. Northeast
Renton 98056
206-235-2352; FAX: 206-235-7832

Seattle Central Community College
1701 Broadway
Seattle 98122-2400
206-587-5425; FAX: 206-344-4323
http://www.seaccd.sccd.ctc.edu/~cculhosp/index.html

Skagit Valley College
2405 College Way
Mount Vernon 98273-5899
360-416-7618; FAX: 360-416-7890

South Puget Sound Community College
2011 Mottman Rd. Southwest
Olympia 98512-6292
360-754-7711; FAX: 360-664-0780
http://www.spscc.ctc.edu

South Seattle Community College
6000 16th Ave. Southwest
Seattle 98106-1499
206-764-5344; FAX: 206-768-6728
http://www.sccd.ctc.edu/

Spokane Community College
1810 North Greene St.
Spokane 99207-5399
509-533-7003; FAX: 509-533-8839

WEST VIRGINIA
Carver Career and Technical
Education Center
4799 Midland Dr.
Charleston 25306
304-348-1965; FAX: 304-348-1938

James Rumsey Technical Institute
Route 6, Box 268
Martinsburg 25401
304-754-7925; FAX: 304-754-7933

Monongalia County Vocational-Technical Center
1000 Mississippi St.
Morgantown 26505
304-292-3361; FAX: 304-291-9247

Shepherd College
Box 268, Route 6
Martinsburg 25401
304-754-5318; Fax: 304-754-7933

West Virginia Northern Community College
1704 Market St.
Wheeling 26003
304-233-5900

WISCONSIN
Blackhawk Technical College
6004 Prairie Rd.
P.O. Box 5009
Janesville 53547-5009
608-757-7713; FAX: 608-757-9407

Chippewa Valley Technical College
620 West Clairemont Ave.
Eau Claire 54701-6120
715-833-6246; FAX: 715-833-6470
http://www.chippewa.tec.wi.us

Fox Valley Technical College
1825 North Bluemound
P.O. Box 2277
Appleton 54913-2277
920-735-5643; FAX: 920-831-5410
http://www.foxvalley.tec.wi.us

Madison Area Technical College
3550 Anderson St.
Madison 53704-2599
608-246-6369; FAX: 608-246-6316
http://www.madison.tec.wi.us/

Milwaukee Area Technical College
700 West State St.
Milwaukee 53233-1443
414-297-6301

Moraine Park Technical College
235 North National Ave.
P.O. Box 1940
Fond du Lac 54936-1940
920-924-3197
http://www.job.careernet.org

Nicolet Area Technical College
Box 518
Rhinelander 54501-0518
715-365-4451; FAX: 715-365-4445
http://www.nicolet.tec.wi.us/

The Postilion School of Culinary Art
220 Old Pioneer Rd.
Fond du Lac 54935
414-922-4170

Waukesha County Technical College
800 Main St.
Pewaukee 53072-4601
414-691-5303; FAX: 414-691-5155

AMERICAN CULINARY FEDERATION APPRENTICESHIPS

ALABAMA
ACF Birmingham Chapter
George White
Jefferson State Community College
2601 Carson Rd.
Birmingham 35215
205-856-7898

ACF Greater Montgomery Chapter
Mary Ann Ward, CEC, CCE
Trenholm State Technical College
1225 Air Base Boulevard
Montgomery 36108
205-262-4728

ALASKA
No listings for this area at this time.

ARIZONA
Chefs Association of Greater Phoenix
Camron Clarkson, CWC
2210 East Sunnyside Dr.
Phoenix 85028
602-706-5004

Chefs Association of South Arizona, Tucson
Ed Doran
4123 East Glenn St.
Tucson 85712
520-881-3408
520-881-7388

Resort and Country Club Chefs of Southwest ACF
Robert J. Chantos, CEC, AAC
Resort and Country Club Chefs Association
P.O. Box 12784
Scottsdale 85267-2784
602-947-9295

ARKANSAS
ACF Central Arkansas Chapter
Sharon B. McCone
24 Fairway Woods Circle
Maumell 72113
501-851-6684

CALIFORNIA
ACF Chefs Association San Joaquin
Bruce Staebler, CEC
1624 Burgan
Clovis 93611
209-434-5750
FAX: 209-434-6160

California Capitol Chefs Association
Jon Greenwalt, CEC, AAC
5475 Asby Lane
Granite Bay 95746
916-791-2554

Chefs de Cuisine Association of California
Leroy Blanchard, CEC
Culinary Arts Department
400 West Washington Boulevard
Los Angeles 90015
213-744-9480
FAX: 213-748-7334

Northern California Chefs Association
Michael Piccinino, CEC, CCE, AAC
6945 Pine Dr.
Anderson 96007
530-225-4829

Orange Empire Chefs Association
Bill Barber, CWC
C/O Orange Coast Community College
2701 Fairview Rd.
P.O. Box 5005
Costa Mesa 92628-5005
714-432-5835

San Francisco Culinary / Pastry Program
Joan Ortega
760 Market St. Ste. 1066
San Francisco 94102
415-989-8726
or
Kay Stickney
855 Oak Grove Ave. #203
Menlo Park 94025
650-327-0585

Santa Clara County Chefs Association
Eric Carter
1572 Monteval Lane
San Jose 95120
408-479-5012

COLORADO
ACF Colorado Chefs de Cuisine
Association Denver
Tiffany Ray
820 16th St., Ste. 421
Denver 80202
303-571-5653
FAX: 303-571-4050
or
Doug Schwartz, CEC
c/o Keystone Resort
Box 38
Dillon 80435
European - Style Apprenticeship
AAS Degree—Culinary Arts
1-800-621-8559
dsch@csn.net
http://www.coloradomtn.edu

ACF Pikes Peak Chapter, Inc.
Siegfried Eisenburger, CEC, AAC
Broadmoor Hotel
1 Lake Ave.
Colorado Springs 80909
719-634-7711 x5336

CONNECTICUT
No listings for this area at this time.

DELAWARE
No listings for this area at this time.

DISTRICT OF COLUMBIA
ACF Nation's Capitol Chefs
Forest Bell
6289 Dunaway Court
McLean 22101
301-469-2018

FLORIDA
ACF Central Florida Chapter
Dale Pennington
Culinary Arts O/TEC
Mid Florida Tech
2900 West Oak Ridge Rd.
Orlando 32809
407-855-5880 x286

ACF First Coast Chapter
John Wright, CEPC, CEC, CCE, AAC
5437 Calloway Court
Jacksonville 32209
904-765-2140

ACF Greater Fort Lauderdale Chapter
Thomas Ferrel
5600 NW 59th St. #1
Tamarac 33319
Beeper 954-848-7133

ACF Gulf to Lakes Chefs and
Cooks Chapter
Steve Neverman
c/o Gulf to Lakes Chapter
P.O. Box 1179
Eustis 32727
352-742-6486
gulfchefs@aol.com

ACF Palm Beach County Chefs
Rod Smith, CEC, AAC
Country Club of Florida
6615 Lawrence Woods Court
Lantana 33462
561-732-2520
FAX: 561-732-7400

ACF Southwest Florida Chefs
Association
Mike Guercio
1625 NE 6th St.
Cape Coral 33909
941-574-7393

ACF Tampa Bay Chefs and Cooks
Association
George Pastor, CEC, CCE, AAC
11722 Spanish Lake Dr.
Tampa 33635-6307
813-932-8612

ACF Treasure Coast Chapter
Thomas Boehm, CWC
Martin County VACE
2801 S. Kanner Highway
Stuart 34994
561-287-0710 x315
or
John Fredericks
Indian River Community College
3209 Virginia Ave.
Fort Pierce 34981-5599
561-462-4225

Disney Culinary Academy
Carolyn Tremblay, Program
Administrator
P. O. Box 10000
Lake Buena Vista 32830-1000
407-827-4701

Gulf Coast Culinary Association
Gus Silivos, CEC
670 Scenic Highway
Pensacola 32503
Work 850-432-6565

Sarasota Bay Chefs Association
Stephen Hodge
8456 Gardens Circle #3
Sarasota 34243
941-355-5151

TC Central Florida—TECOM
Rick Petrello, CEC, CCE, AAC
2900 West Oakridge Rd.
Orlando 32809
407-344-5080

Volusia County Chefs and Cooks
Jeff Conklin
Daytona Beach Community College
1200 West International Boulevard
Daytona Beach 32120
904-255-8131 x3735

GEORGIA
ACF Augusta Chapter
Harry Sayles, CEC
2010 Bald Eagle Dr.
Hephzibah 30815
706-722-3008

ACF Golden Isles of Georgia
Charles Miller
504 E. Island Square
St. Simons Island
912-638-3611

ACF Inc. Chefs Association of Greater
Atlanta
John Brantley, CEC
3571 Forrest Glen Trail
Lawrenceville 30244
770-495-0997

HAWAII
Chefs de Cuisine Association of Hawaii
Randy Francisco
Kapiolani Community College OCS
1424 Diamond Rd.
Honolulu 96816
808-734-9457

Maui Chefs Association
Christopher Speere
C/O Maui Community College
310 Kaahumanu Ave.
P.O. Box 1284
Haiku 96708
808-242-1210

IDAHO
No listings for this area at this time.

ILLINOIS
ACF Chef de Cuisine / Quad Cities
(Iowa)
Brad Scott
Scott Community College
500 Belmont Rd.
Bettendorf 52722
319-359-7531 x278

ACF Chicago Chefs of Cuisine, Inc.
Edward R. Krause
8536 W 95th St. Apt 10
Hickory Hills 60457
708-429-7400

INDIANA
ACF Greater Indianapolis Chapter
Allen Elsesy, CEC
P. O. Box 355
St. Paul 47242
317-615-1510 x220

ACF South Bend Chapter
Denis F. Ellis, CEC, AAC
University of Notre Dame
South Dining Hall
Notre Dame 46556
219-631-5416

IOWA
ACF Greater Des Moines Culinary
Association
Robert Anderson
Des Moines Area Community College
2006 South Ankeny Boulevard
Andeny 50021
515-964-6200 x6566

KANSAS
ACF Greater Kansas City Chef's
Association
Patrick Sweeney, CEC, AAC
Johnson County Community College
12345 College at Quivira
Overland Park, Kansas 66210
913-469-8500 x3611

KENTUCKY
No listings for this area at this time.

LOUISIANA
ACF New Orleans Chapter
Iva Bergeron, CCE
Delgado Community College
615 City Park Ave., Bldg. 11
New Orleans 70119-4399
504-483-4208

MAINE
No listings for this area at this time.

MARYLAND
Central Maryland Chefs Association
Terry Green, CCE
Western School
100 Kenwood
Baltimore 21228
410-887-0852
or
Elaine Madden
C-205
101 College Parkway
Arnold 21012
410-541-2550

MASSACHUSETTS
Epicurean Club of Boston
Christoph Leu
The Westin Hotel
10 Huntington Ave.
Boston 02116-5798
617-424-7524

Massachusetts Culinary Association
Stanley Nicas, CEC AAC
1230 Main St.
Leicester 01524
508-892-9090

MICHIGAN
ACF Blue Water Chefs Association
David F. Schneider, CEC, CCE
Macomb Community College
44575 Garfield Rd.
Clinton Township 48038-1139
810-286-2088
FAX: 810-286-2038

ACF Michigan Chefs de Cuisine
Association
Kevin Enright, CEC, CCE
Oakland Community College
27055 Orchard Lake Rd.
Farmington Hills 48334-4579
248-471-7786

ACF of Nortwestern Michigan
Andrew Colvin, CC
Shanty Creek - Schuss Mountain
Bellair 49615
616-533-8621

MINNESOTA
No listings for this area at this time.

MISSISSIPPI
No listings for this area at this time.

MISSOURI
ACF Chefs and Cooks of Springfield /
Ozark
James Lekander, CEC
707 McLean Court
Nixa 65714
417-724-0968

Chefs De Cuisine of St. Louis
Michael Downey
St. Louis Community College
5600 Oaksland Ave., HRM Department
St. Louis 63110
314-664-9100

MONTANA
No listings for this area at this time.

NEBRASKA
ACF Professional Chefs of Omaha
Jim Trebbien, CCE
Metropolitan Community College
Bldg. 10
P.O. Box 3777, 30th and Fort Streets
Omaha 68103-0777
402-457-2510
FAX: 402-457-2515

NEVADA
The Fraternity of Executive Chefs of
Las Vegas ACF
Joseph Mulligan, CEC
132 Villaggio
Henderson 89014
702-435-3206

High Sierra Chefs Association
Paul J. Lee, CWC
Harrah's Lake Tahoe
P.O. Box 8
Lake Tahoe 89449
702-588-6611

NEW HAMPSHIRE
Greater Northern New Hampshire
Phil Learned, CEC AAC
The Balsams Resort Hotel
Box 112
Dixville Notch 03576
603-255-3861

NEW JERSEY

ACF Northern New Jersey Chapter
Joe Amabile, CEC
Bergan County Tech High School
200 Hackensack Ave.
Hackensack 07601
201-343-6000 x2255

Professional Chefs Guild of Central
New Jersey
Doug Fee
Mercer County Community College
1200 Old Trenton Rd.
Trenton 08690
609-586-4800 x3476

Professional Chefs of South Jersey
John Carbone, CCE, CEC, AAC
P.O. Box 157
Port Republic 08241
609-646-4950

NEW MEXICO

ACF Chefs of Santa Fe
Maurice Zeck, CEC, AAC
100 East San Francisco St.
Santa Fe 87501
505-982-5511

ACF Rio Grande Valley Chapter
Diane Ciampolillo, CEC
Albuquerque Tech-Vocational Inst.
920 River View Dr. SE
Rio Rancho 87124
505-896-3000
FAX: 505-896-4205

ACF Southwest New Mexico and Texas
Tatsuya Miyazaki
930 El Paseo Rd.
Las Cruces 88001
505-526-7144

NEW YORK

ACF Capital District of Central New York
Scott A. Vadney
43 Berwyn St.
Schenectady 12304
518-797-3222
FAX: 518-797-3692
capdistchefs@juno.net

ACF of Greater Buffalo New York
Samuel J. Sheusi, CEC, CCE
5084 Dana Dr.
Lewiston 14092
716-731-4101

Mid-Hudson Culinary Association
Brent Wertz, CWC
Mohonk Mountain House
Lake Mohonk
New Paltz 12561
914-256-2070
FAX: 914-256-2161

NORTH CAROLINA

ACF Inc. Charlotte Chapter
Chris Jones
P.O. Box 471053
Charlotte 28248
704-597-0414
or
Phillip Lloyd
704-892-6461

ACF Sandhills / Cross Creek Chefs
Association
Paul Ramsey, CEC
Pinehurst Resort
P.O. Box 4000 Carolina Vista
Village of Pinehurst 28374
919-295-8439

Triad Professional Chefs Association
S Mitchell Mack
C/O HIFS
3121 High Point Rd.
Greesboro 27407
919-242-9161 x4112

Western North Carolina Culinary
Association
Dennis R. Trantham, CC
Route 4, Box 256A
Canton 28716
704-648-7195

NORTH DAKOTA
No listings for this area at this time.

OHIO
ACF Cleveland Chapter
Richard Fulchiron, CEC
or Jan Delucia
Cuyahoga Community College
Metropolitan Campus
2900 Community College Ave.
Cleveland 44115
216-987-4087
216-987-4082
Email: richardfulchiron@tri_c.cc.oh.us

ACF Columbus Chefs Chapter
Carol Kizer, CCE
Columbus State Community College
550 East Spring St.
Columbus 43215
614-227-2579

OKLAHOMA
ACF Culinary Arts of Oklahoma
Genni Thomas, CEPC CEC CCE AAC
4337 Dahoon Dr.
Oklahoma City 73120
405-749-3155
FAX: 405-749-3214

ACF Tulsa Chapter
Robert M. Boyce, CWC
5531 South Toledo Place
Tulsa 74135-4325
918-486-6575
FAX: 918-486-6576

OREGON
No listings for this area at this time.

PENNSYLVANIA
ACF Laurel Highlands Chapter
Mary Zappone, CCE
Westmoreland Community College
Culinary Arts
Armbrust Rd.
Youngwood 15697-1895
412-925-4016

ACF Pittsburgh Chapter
Paul Passafume
274 Washington St.
Whitacre 15120
412-578-5513

Delaware Valley Chefs Association
William Tillinghast
3191 Janney St.
Philadelphia 19134
215-895-1143

Southern Allegheny Chefs Association
Doug Simon
RD 1 Box 624
Bedford 15522
Chapter Office 814-684-9490

RHODE ISLAND
No listings for this area at this time.

SOUTH CAROLINA
ACF Midland Chapter
Bruce A. Sacino, CEC
800 Richland street
Columbia 29201
803-737-6574
FAX: 803-737-2342
Email: scsacino@aol.com

SOUTH DAKOTA
No listings for this area at this time.

TENNESSEE
ACF Middle Tennessee Chapter,
Opryland Hotel
Dina D. Starks, RD
2800 Opryland Dr.
Nashville 37214
615-871-7765

TEXAS
ACF Capitol of Texas Chefs
Matt Collins, CWC
c/o ACF Capital of Texas Chefs
6020 Dilliard Circle
Austin 78752
512-323-2511

ACF Professional Chefs Association of
Houston
Dan Capello
The Houston Country Club
1 Potomac Dr.
Houston 77057
713-465-8381 x246
FAX: 713-465-7455

TCA—Brazos Valley Chapter
Vicki Beck
Texas A & M
Foodservice Department
College Station 77843

TCA—Dallas
James Goering, CCE, CEC
El Centro College
Main at Lamar
Dallas 75202-9604
214-746-2217

TCA—Houston
George Messinger
19826 Atascicota Pines Dr.
Humble 74346
713-459-7150

Texas Chefs Association
George J. Messinger, CEC, CCE
19826 Atascocita Pines Dr.
Humble 77346
281-459-7150

UTAH
No listings for this area at this time.

VERMONT
North Vermont Chefs and Cooks
Association
Patrick R. Miller, CEC
2575 Weeks Hill Rd.
Stowe 05672
802-253-4236

VIRGINIA
Blue Ridge Chefs Association
Bill King, CEC
3425 Pippin Lane
Charlottesville 22903
703-894-5436
FAX: 703-894-0534

Virgina Chefs Association
Bruce Clarke
3204 Old Gun Rd. East
Midlothian 23113
804-272-0761

WASHINGTON
Washington State Chefs Association
Jamie Callison, CC
8720 231st St. SW
Edmonds 98026
206-363-2169

WEST VIRGINIA
ACF West Virginia Chapter
Dan Ferguson, CWC
216 Rockledge Dr.
Nitro 25143
304-776-3559

WISCONSIN
ACF Chefs of Milwaukee, Inc.
John Reiss
Milwaukee Area Technical College
700 West State St.
Milwaukee 53233
414-297-6861
or
Jim Holden
Waukesha County Technical College
800 Main St.
Pewaukee 53072
414-691-5303

ACF Fox Valley Chapter
Albert Exenberger, CEC, CCE, AAC
Fox Valley Technical Institute
1825 North Bluemound Dr.
P.O. Box 2277
Appleton 54913-2277
414-735-5600 x735

ACF Middle Wisconsin Chefs
Gregory Krzyminski
Mid-state Technical College
500 32nd St. North
Wisconsin Rapids 54494
715-423-5650

WYOMING
No listings for this area at this time.

THE INSIDE TRACK

Who:	Mike Nipper
What:	Island Clubhouse Chef
Where:	The Westin Innisbrook Resort, Palm Harbor
How long:	One-and-a-half years in current position; thirteen years in the Food and Beverage Industry

Insider's Advice

You have to be dedicated to this profession if you want to succeed. To me, it's a passion. I love food, and I've always put artistic expression into my food presentations to make them unique to my style of cooking. A common saying is that you don't pick this business, it picks you. And it is something you have to love. If you don't love it, you probably won't make it because the demands are incredible. For instance, you may be separated from your family, have to work 14-16 hours some days, and work on holidays. You have to be aware of what you're getting into before you come into this field. It almost seems like you have to be a compulsive, obsessive, type-A personality to succeed.

Before you head off to culinary school, take the time to really think about the career and decide if it's something you can dedicate your life to. If so, you need to actually work in the industry for a couple years. And you can't work just any place—you need to pick an established, well-known restaurant where a talented chef is in charge of the kitchen, so you can get a really good grasp of the fundamentals. Learn the basics, such as how to make a good stock, because if you don't have a good stock, then you can't make a good sauce. After working in a good restaurant for a few years, attend a culinary program at either a community college, local vocational school, or one of the top culinary schools. You can learn a lot in a good culinary program, and I definitely advise you to enroll in one.

Be aware that you have to put your time in and pay your dues. Don't think it's going to be easy or that as soon as you graduate from culinary school you'll be a great chef who gets on television or a chef who gets to write for the glossy food magazines. In fact, you don't graduate culinary school as a *chef.* You graduate with the *tools* to become a chef. Then it's up to you to live up to your potential by taking what you learn in culinary school and working with it to succeed.

Insider's Take on the Future

I think we'll see a more conscious culinary field—chefs and cooks who are more environmentally conscious and health conscious. Indeed, more chefs are getting involved in recycling and in purchasing ingredients from local farmers. Also, we are using more organic goods in the industry than we have previously and more farmers and chefs are building partnerships. I buy products from people in the community whenever possible. One good thing we have right on our property here at Innisbrook is an herb garden. So I can tell a customer that the sage or parsley on her plate was just picked this morning.

CHAPTER | 4

This chapter covers how to receive financial aid for the training program you want to attend. You'll find out how to determine your eligibility for financial aid, distinguish among the different types of aid, gather your financial records, and file your forms once you have completed them. A sample financial aid form is included.

FINANCIAL AID FOR THE TRAINING YOU NEED

Culinary training programs can be expensive, so you need a plan for financing your training. That is what this chapter is all about. You can qualify for financial aid at many different types of schools, including community and technical colleges, universities, vocational schools, and culinary institutes. Many types of financial aid may also be used to help you pay for short-term training programs or certificates. You can often qualify for some type of financial aid even if you're only attending school half-time—the financial aid you'll get may be less than in full-time programs, but it can still be worthwhile and help you pay for a portion of your training program.

ENTERING THE WORLD OF FINANCIAL AID

Don't let financial aid anxiety deter you from finding out more about the many options you have for financing your culinary arts training program. You can get a good overview of the whole process in the time it takes you to read this chapter. Plus, resources are listed at the end of the chapter so you can get even more information. Additionally, most schools have financial aid advisors who can address your concerns and help you fill out the necessary paperwork. So there is no shortage of information available to help you. Take advantage of it today!

EXPOSING FINANCIAL AID MYTHS

The financial aid process is not as confusing as many people think it is. It is a process with a set of ordered and logical steps. So don't be taken in by any of the myths you hear about financial aid. One of the most common myths is that the only type of financial aid that most students get is a burdensome loan, or a job from a work-study program that will lead to burnout and poor grades. The truth is that in addition to federal and state financial aid, most schools offer their own grants and scholarships. Other students win scholarships from one or more of the culinary organizations listed in this chapter.

The reality is that you can probably get a combination of scholarships, loans, and work-study. As for working while in school, it's true that it is a challenge to hold down a full-time or even part-time job while in school, but a moderate amount of work-study employment while attending classes (10–12 hours per week) can actually improve academic performance because it forces students to hone their time-management skills. Indeed, due to the high costs of many culinary programs, you'll find that most students hold down either a part-time or full-time job while they attend school. In fact, many chefs recommend that students work in the industry while they are attending classes, so they can practice the techniques they are learning in school.

A second common myth concerns the terminology of the financial aid process. People think that the financial aid process is too difficult to understand because of all the unfamiliar terms and strange acronyms that are used. At first, the jargon of financial aid can be confusing, but with a little practice, you'll be fluent in no time. While you will encounter an amazing number of acronyms and some unfamiliar terms while applying for financial aid, as you progress through the process, these terms will actually become quite familiar to you. For additional help, refer to the handy acronyms key and glossary at the end of this chapter.

GETTING STARTED

The first step in the financial aid process is to get a form that is called *Free Application for Federal Student Aid* (FAFSA). You can get this form from several sources: your public library, your school's financial aid office, or by calling 1-800-4-FED-AID. You need to get an original form to mail in because photocopies of federal forms are not acceptable. If you are computer savvy and have access to the Internet, you can visit a Web site at http://www.finaid.org/finaid.html, where you fill out and submit the form on-line. You'll need to print out, sign, and send in the release and signature pages.

In financial aid circles, this form is commonly referred to by its initials: FAFSA. The FAFSA determines your eligibility status for all grants and loans provided by federal or state governments and certain college or institution aid; it is the first step in the financial aid process, and it should be done as soon as possible. Many school-based or private aid sources require students to complete a FAFSA in order to become eligible for their financial aid packages.

The second step is to create a financial aid calendar. You can use any standard calendar—wall, desk, or portable—for this task. The main thing is to write all of the application deadlines for each step of the financial aid process on one calendar, so you can see at a glance what needs to be done at what time. You can start this calendar by writing in the date you requested your FAFSA. Then mark down when you received it and when you sent the completed form in. Add important dates and deadlines for any other applications you need to complete for school-based or private aid as you progress though the financial aid process. Using and maintaining a calendar will help the whole financial aid process run more smoothly and give you peace of mind that the important dates are written down and are not merely bouncing around in your head.

Determining Your Eligibility

To receive federal financial aid from an accredited college or institution's student aid program, you must:

* have a high school diploma or a General Education Development (GED) certificate, pass a test approved by the U.S. Department of Education, or meet other standards your state establishes that are approved by the U.S. Department of Education

- be enrolled or accepted for enrollment as a regular student working toward a degree or certificate in an eligible program
- be a U.S. citizen or eligible noncitizen and have a valid social security number
- make satisfactory academic progress
- sign a statement of educational purpose and a certification statement on overpayment and default
- register with selective services, if required
- have financial need, except for some loan and other aid programs

You are eligible to apply for federal financial aid by completing the FAFSA even if you haven't yet been accepted to or enrolled in a school. However, you do need to be enrolled in an accredited training program in order to actually receive any funds from a federal financial aid program.

Apply Early

Apply for financial aid as soon as possible after January 1st of the year in which you want to enroll in school. For example, if you want to begin school in the fall of 1999, then you should apply for financial aid as soon as possible after January 1, 1999. It is easier to complete the FAFSA after you have completed your tax return, so you may want to consider filing your taxes as early as possible as well. Do not sign, date, or send your FAFSA before January 1st of the year for which you are seeking aid. Applications are accepted from January 1st to June 30th each year, so be sure to make the deadline. If you apply by mail, send your completed application in the envelope that came with the original application. The envelope is already addressed, and using it will make sure your application reaches the correct address. Many students lose out on thousands of dollars in grants and loans because they file too late. Don't be one of those students!

After you mail in your completed FAFSA, your application will be processed in approximately four weeks. Then, you will receive a Student Aid Report (SAR) in the mail. The SAR will report the information from your application and, if there are no questions or problems with your application, your SAR will report your Expected Family Contribution (EFC), the number used to determine your eligibility for federal student aid. Each school you list on the application may also receive your application information if the school is set up to receive the information electronically.

You must reapply for financial aid every year. However, after your first year, you will receive a Student Aid Report (SAR) in the mail before the application deadline. If no corrections need to be made, you can just sign it and send it in.

How to File Your Forms

1. Get an original Federal Application for Federal Student Aid (FAFSA). Remember to pick up an original copy of this form as photocopies are not acceptable.

2. Fill out the entire FAFSA as completely as possible. Make an appointment with a financial aid counselor if you need help. Read the forms completely, and don't skip any relevant portions.

3. Return the FAFSA before the deadline date. Financial aid counselors warn that many students don't file the forms before the deadline and lose out on available aid.

FINANCIAL NEED

Financial aid from many of the programs discussed in this chapter is awarded on the basis of financial need (except for unsubsidized Stafford, PLUS, and Consolidation loans, and some scholarships and grants). When you apply for federal student aid by completing the FAFSA, the information you report is used in a formula established by the U.S. Congress. The formula determines your Expected Family Contribution (EFC), an amount you and your family are expected to contribute toward your education. If your EFC is below a certain amount, you'll be eligible for a federal Pell grant, assuming you meet all other eligibility requirements.

There isn't a maximum EFC that defines eligibility for the other financial aid options. Instead, your EFC is used in an equation to determine your financial needs.

Cost of Attendance – Expected Family Contribution = Financial Need

---

A financial aid administrator calculates your cost of attendance and subtracts the amount you and your family are expected to contribute toward that cost. If there's anything left over, you're considered to have financial need.

Are You Considered Dependent or Independent?

You need to find out if you are considered to be a dependent or an independent student by the federal government. Federal policy uses strict and specific criteria to make this designation. A dependent student is expected to have parental contribution to school expenses, and an independent student is not. The parental contribution depends on the number of parents with earned income, the amount of income and assets, the age of the older parent, the family size, and the number of family members enrolled in post-secondary education. Income is not merely the adjusted gross income from the tax return, but also includes nontaxable income such as social security benefits and child support.

You're considered to be an independent student if at least one of the following applies to you:

- you are 24 years old
- you are married (even if you're separated)
- you have legal dependents other than a spouse who get more than half of their support from you and will continue to get that support during the award year
- you are an orphan or ward of the court (or were a ward of the court until age 18)
- you are a graduate or professional student
- you are a veteran of the U.S. Armed Forces—formerly engaged in active service in the U.S. Army, Navy, Air Force, Marines, or Coast Guard or as a cadet or midshipman at one of the service academies—released under a condition other than dishonorable.

If you live with your parents and they claimed you as a dependent on their last tax return, then your need will be based on your parents' income. However, you do not qualify for independent status just because your parents have decided not to claim you as an exemption on their tax return (this used to be the case but is no longer) or do not want to provide financial support for your college education.

Students are classified as dependent or independent because federal student aid programs are based on the idea that students (and their parents or spouse, if applicable) have the primary responsibility for paying for their post-secondary education.

Gathering Financial Records

Your financial need for most grants and loans depends on your financial situation. Now that you've determined if you are considered a dependent or independent student, you'll know whose financial records you need to gather for this step of the process. If you are a dependent student, then you must gather not only your own financial records, but those of your parents also because you must report their income and assets as well as your own when you complete the FAFSA. If you are an independent student, then you need to gather only your own financial records (and those of your spouse if you're married). Find your tax records from the year previous to when you are applying. For example, if you apply for the fall of 1999, you will use your tax records for the 1998 year.

To help you fill out the FAFSA, gather the following financial records:

* U.S. Income Tax Returns (IRS Form 1040, 1040A, or 1040EZ) for the year that just ended and W-2 and 1099 forms
* records of untaxed income, such as Social Security benefits, AFDC or ADC, child support, welfare, pensions, military subsistence allowances, or veterans benefits
* current bank statements and mortgage information
* medical and dental expenses for the past year that weren't covered by health insurance
* business and/or farm records
* records of investments such as stocks, bonds, and mutual funds, as well as bank Certificates of Deposit (CDs) and recent statements from money market accounts
* Social Security number(s)

Even if you do not complete your federal income tax return until March or April, you should not wait to file your FAFSA until your tax returns are filed with the IRS. Instead, use estimated income information and submit the FAFSA, as noted below, just as soon as possible after January 1st. Be as accurate as possible, but you can correct estimates later.

TYPES OF FINANCIAL AID

There are many types of financial aid available to help with school expenses. Three general categories exist for financial aid:

1. grants and scholarships—aid that you don't have to pay back
2. work/study—aid that you earn by working
3. loans—aid that you have to pay back

Grants

Grants are a great form of financial aid because they do not need to be paid back. They are normally awarded based on financial need. Here are the two most common forms of grants for undergraduate students:

Federal Pell Grants

Federal Pell grants are based on financial need and are awarded only to undergraduate students who have not yet earned a bachelor's or professional degree. Almost four million students get a Pell grant every year. For many students, Pell grants provide a foundation of financial aid to which other aid may be added. Awards for the award year will depend on program funding. The maximum award for the 1998-1999 award year was $3,000. You can receive only one Pell grant in an award year, and you may not receive Pell grant funds for more than one school at a time.

How much you get will depend not only on your Expected Family Contribution (EFC) but on your cost of attendance, whether you're a full-time or half-time student, and whether you attend school for a full academic year or less. You can qualify for a Pell grant even if you are only enrolled half-time in a training program. You should also be aware that some private and school-based sources of financial aid will not consider your eligibility if you haven't first applied for a Pell grant.

Chef Sharon Odmann knows the value of applying for a Pell grant firsthand. She describes her experience of deciding which culinary school to attend and how it worked out for her:

> Someone mentioned to me that I should go to a culinary school. I knew about the Culinary Institute of America and Johnson & Wales, but they are so expensive; plus I didn't want to relocate my family. So I had an interview at a community college in Harrisburg, Pennsylvania—and my age was a good factor because they knew I wasn't going to be bouncing in and out of school (I was 43 at the time). I was able to get Pell grants, so the whole program didn't cost me very much, and I graduated with an associate degree in culinary arts.

Federal Supplemental Educational Opportunity Grants (FSEOG)

A Federal Supplemental Educational Opportunity Grant (FSEOG) is for undergraduates with exceptional financial need—that is, students with the lowest

Expected Family Contributions (EFCs). It gives priority to students who receive federal Pell grants. An FSEOG is similar to a Pell grant in that it doesn't need to be paid back.

You can receive between $100 and $4,000 a year, depending on when you apply, your level of need, and the funding level of the school you're attending. There's no guarantee every eligible student will be able to receive an FSEOG. Students at each school are paid based on the availability of funds at that school, and not all schools participate in this program. To increase your chances of getting this grant, apply as early as you can after January 1st of the year in which you plan to attend school.

Scholarships

You can obtain scholarships from federal, state, school, and private sources. The best aspect of scholarships is that you don't have to pay them back! To find private sources of aid, spend a few hours in the library or bookstore looking at scholarship and fellowship books. See the *Resources* section at the end of this chapter to find relevant scholarship book titles. If you're currently employed, check to see if your employer has scholarship funds or tuition reimbursement programs available. If you're a dependent student, ask your parents and aunts, uncles, and cousins to check with their employers or organizations they belong to for possible aid sources. You never know what type of private aid you might dig up. For example, any of the following groups may know of money that could be yours:

- professional culinary associations
- religious organizations
- fraternal organizations
- clubs, such as the Rotary, Kiwanas, American Legion, or 4H
- athletic clubs
- veterans groups
- ethnic group associations
- unions

Jennifer McAllister, a student in the Pastry and Baking program at Peter Kump's New York Cooking School, offers this advice to prospective students:

> Apply for all the scholarships you can find. I applied for scholarships
> from the International Association of Culinary Professionals (IACP)

and the James Beard Foundation. I found out that I was a finalist for three scholarships through these foundations, and I won them all. About 90% of my tuition was paid for, so I did not have to go heavily into debt by taking on a large loan.

When applying for a scholarship, try to convey your enthusiasm for your work. You'll either write an essay explaining why you are applying for a scholarship and why you are pursuing a culinary arts career, or you'll be interviewed over the telephone. So let your passion for the work shine through.

If you have already selected the school you will attend, check with a financial aid administrator (FAA) to find out if you qualify for any school-based scholarships or other aid. To attract more students to their school, many schools now offer merit-based aid for students with a high school GPA of a certain level or with a certain level of SAT scores. Also check with the culinary arts department to see if they have a bulletin board or other method of posting available scholarships that are specific to culinary arts programs.

It pays to do some research on scholarships, as culinary arts professional Kim O'Donnel learned firsthand. She spent time investigating cooking schools and ways to finance her tuition. She says:

> I found out that Peter Kump's New York Cooking School has a work-study program that allows you to work as an assistant in any area of the school for a semester; then, the next semester you get to take classes. However, at the same time, I won a memorial scholarship from the James Beard Foundation that was earmarked for Peter Kump's. It was a full scholarship, and it was perfect timing. The program was 20 weeks long (14 weeks in class and a six-week externship), so I was able to go to school for a reasonable amount of time.

As you look for sources of scholarships, continue to enhance your chances of winning one by participating in extracurricular events and volunteer activities. You should also obtain references from people who know you well and are leaders in the community, so you can submit their names or letters of recommendation with your scholarship applications. Make a list of any awards you've received or other special honors that you could list on your scholarship application.

Here are several culinary arts scholarships that you might be eligible for.

American Culinary Federation Scholarships

The American Culinary Federation is one of the largest professional culinary associations, and it has many local chapters throughout America. To find out information about both national and local scholarships, contact the American Culinary Federation, P.O. Box 3466, St. Augustine, FL 32085; the phone number is 800-624-9458.

American Institute of Baking Scholarships

Scholarships are offered by the American Institute of Baking to students in culinary training programs. Contact them for more information at the American Institute of Baking, P.O. Box 3999, Manhattan, KS 66505-3999; the phone number is 785-537-4750.

American Institute of Wine and Food Scholarships

The American Institute of Wine and Food has funds available for scholarships through their local chapters. Contact their headquarters for more information at the American Institute of Wine and Food (AIWF), 1550 Bryant Street, Suite 700, San Francisco, CA 94103; the phone number is 415-255-3000 or 800-274-2493.

American Society for Hospital Food Service Administrators Scholarships

The American Society for Hospital Food Service Administrators offers up to $1,000 for full- or part-time students of institutional foodservice management. They have three scholarship funds: one is for undergraduates at both two- and four-year colleges, and the other two are for continuing education for current hospital foodservice managers. For more information, contact the Scholarship Committee, American Society for Hospital Food Service Administrators, American Hospital Association, 840 North Lake Shore Drive, Chicago, IL 60611; the phone number is 312-280-0000.

Careers through Culinary Arts Program Scholarships

Scholarships are available for high school students at participating high across the nation. Check with your local guidance counselor or home economics teacher to find out if your school participates in the CCAP program or contact the national office at Careers Through Culinary Arts Program, 155 West 68th Street, New York, NY 10023; the phone number is 212-873-2434.

Confrérie de la Chaîne des Rôtisseurs Scholarships

The Chaîne Foundation is a tax-exempt organization that supports culinary education programs in keeping with the goals of Confrérie de la Chaîne des Rôtisseurs, Bailliage des Etats-Unis. Scholarships are available directly from selected culinary schools through this program. You'll need to ask the financial aid administrator at each school you are considering to find out if that school has information about these scholarships. Two schools that have these scholarships are the Culinary Institute of America and Johnson & Wales University. Other schools may also be involved with scholarships from this foundation. For more information, contact Confrérie de la Chaîne des Rôtisseurs, 444 Park Avenue South, Suite 301, New York, NY 10016–7321; the phone number is 212-683-3770.

Educational Foundation of the National Restaurant Association Scholarships

The Educational Foundation of the National Restaurant Association (EF of NRA) offers several different scholarships for students specializing in foodservice, hospitality management, culinary arts, food technology, dietetics, and related areas. The undergraduate scholarship requires that you have a minimum of six months' foodservice work experience. You can find out the amount of each award by contacting the Scholarship Department, Educational Foundation of the National Restaurant Association, 250 South Wacker Drive, Suite 1400, Chicago, IL 60606; the phone number is 312-715-1010.

Hospitality Sales and Marketing Association Chapter Scholarships

When funds are available in certain regional chapters, the Hospitality Sales and Marketing Association International (HSMAI) may offer limited types of scholarships to students in the hospitality industry. Contact the headquarters office for more information at Hospitality Sales and Marketing Association International (HSMAI), 1300 L Street NW, Suite 800, Washington, DC 20005; the phone number is 202-789-0089.

International Association of Culinary Professionals Foundation Scholarships

The International Association of Culinary Professionals Foundation awards approximately 50 different scholarships in the form of partial or full tuition payment or cash awards. Some of the scholarships are awarded to students attending a particular culinary program and others are for students to use in any culinary program of their choice. Both beginning and continuing education awards are available. Approximately $220,000 in scholarships has been awarded for the 1998-1999 school year. Finalists are interviewed by telephone.

Applicants must fill out an application form and submit an essay stating their culinary aspirations and goals. They must also submit transcripts of academic work (if completed within the past 10 years) and the names of two people who can be asked for professional recommendations. To find out more information about these scholarships, contact the International Association of Culinary Professionals Foundation, 304 W. Liberty Street, Suite 201, Louisville, KY 40202; the phone number is 502-587-7953 or 800-928-4227.

International Food Service Executives Scholarships

The International Food Service Executives Association (IFSEA) awards annually two scholarships ranging from $250 to $500 in each of eight regions to foodservice-related majors. Many local branches also offer annual scholarships to student members, totaling almost $100,000 nationwide. For more information, contact the International Food Service Executives Association, 1100 South State Road 7, Suite 103, Margate, FL 33068; the phone number is 305-977-0767.

James Beard Foundation Scholarships

The James Beard Foundation offers a number of scholarships for culinary education every year. The current deadline is March 1st of each year. For more information, contact the James Beard Foundation Scholarships, 167 W. 12th Street, New York, NY 10011; the phone number is 212-675-4984 or 800-36BEARD.

National Association for the Specialty Food Trade Scholarships

The National Association for the Specialty Food Trade has a scholarship and research fund that offers scholarships to culinary students. For more information, contact them at the National Association for the Specialty Food Trade, Scholarship Department, 120 Wall Street, 27th floor, New York, NY 10005-4001; the phone number is 212-482-6440.

Women Chefs and Restaurateurs Scholarships

The Women Chefs and Restaurateurs Association awards grants and scholarships on a limited basis. To find out more, contact them at the Women Chefs and Restaurateurs, 110 Sutter Street, #210, San Francisco, CA 94104; the phone number is 415-362-7336.

Culinary Scoop

Who was James Beard? James Beard is recognized as the father of American gastronomy. Throughout his life, he pursued innovation in the culinary arts and acted as a mentor to emerging talents.

Work-Study Programs

A variety of work-study programs are available as a form of financial aid. If you already know which school you want to attend, you can find out about its school-based work-study options from the student employment office. Job possibilities may include on- or off-campus jobs either in the culinary arts field or an unrelated area. Another type of work-study program is called the Federal Work-Study (FWS) program and it can be applied for on the FAFSA.

The Federal Work-Study program provides jobs for undergraduate and graduate students *with financial need* allowing them to earn money to help pay education expenses. The program encourages community service work and provides hands-on experience related to a student's course of study, when available. The amount of the FWS award depends on:

* when you apply (again, *apply early*)
* your level of financial need
* the funds that are available at your particular school

Your FWS salary will be at least the current federal minimum wage or higher depending on the type of work you do and the skills required. As an undergraduate, you'll be paid by the hour (a graduate student may receive a salary), and you will receive the money directly from your school at least monthly. The awards are not transferable from year to year, and not all schools participate in the FWS program. You will be assigned a job on campus, in a private non-profit organization, or a public agency that offers a public service. The total hourly wages you earn in each year cannot exceed your total FWS award for that year, and you cannot work more than 20 hours per week.

If you cannot finance your entire training program through scholarships, grants, or work-study exclusively, the next step is to consider taking out a loan. Be cautious about the amount you borrow, but remember that it may be worth it to borrow money to attend a training program that will enhance your future job prospects.

Student Loans

The first step in finding a student loan is to learn the basics of loan programs. You need to become familiar with several student loan programs, especially the federal government loans. You can get a good start on this process by reading the rest of this chapter. To get more detailed information than appears here, seek guidance from a financial aid administrator or banking institution.

Questions to Ask Before You Take out a Loan

Here are a few sample questions you might want to ask before you take out a loan, along with tips to help you get the information you need.

1. *What is the interest rate and how often is the interest capitalized?* Your college's financial aid administrator or a lender may be able to tell you this.
2. *What fees will be charged?* Government loans generally have an origination fee that goes to the federal government to help offset its costs, and a guarantee fee, which goes to a guarantee agency for insuring the loan. Both are deducted from the amount given to you.
3. *Will I have to make any payments while still in school?* Usually you won't, and, depending on the type of loan, the government may even pay the interest for you while you're in school.
4. *What is the grace period—the period after my schooling ends, during which no payment is required?* You need to find out if it is long enough, realistically, for you to find a job and get on your feet. (A six-month grace period is common.)
5. *When will my first payment be due and approximately how much will it be?* You can get a good preview of the repayment process from the answer to this question.
6. *Will I have the right to pre-pay my loan, without penalty, at any time?* Some loan programs allow pre-payment with no penalty, but others do not.
7. *Will deferments and forbearances be possible if I am temporarily unable to make payments?* You need to find out how to apply for a deferment or forbearance if you need it.

Federal Perkins Loans

A federal Perkins loan has the lowest interest rate (approximately 5%) of any loan available, and it is offered to students with exceptional financial need. You repay your school, who lends the money to you with government funds.

Depending on when you apply, your level of need, and the funding level of the school, you can borrow up to $3,000 for each year of undergraduate study for up to five years.

The school pays you directly by check or credits your tuition account. You have nine months after you graduate (provided you were continuously enrolled at least half-time) to begin repayment, with up to 10 years to pay off the entire loan.

Parent Loan for Undergraduate Students (PLUS)

PLUS loans enable parents with good credit histories to borrow money to pay the education expenses of a child who is a dependent undergraduate student enrolled at least half-time. To be eligible, your parents must meet citizenship requirements and pass a credit check. If they don't pass the credit check, they might still be able to receive a loan if they can show that extenuating circumstances exist or if someone who is able to pass the credit check agrees to co-sign the loan.

The annual limit on a PLUS loan is equal to your cost of attendance minus any other financial aid you receive. For instance, if your cost of attendance is $6,000 and you receive $2,000 in other financial aid, your parents could borrow up to, but no more than, $4,000. The interest rate varies, but is not to exceed 9% over the life of the loan. Your parents must begin repayment while you're still in school—there is no grace period.

Federal Stafford Loans

Federal Stafford loans are low interest loans, and you must attend school at least half-time to be eligible. The lender of the loan is usually a bank or credit union; however, sometimes a school may be the lender. Stafford loans are either subsidized or unsubsidized.

- **Subsidized loans** are awarded on the basis of financial need. You will not be charged any interest before you begin repayment or during authorized periods of deferment. The federal government "subsidizes" the interest during these periods.
- **Unsubsidized loans** are not awarded on the basis of financial need. You'll be charged interest from the time the loan is disbursed until it is paid in full. If you allow the interest to accumulate, it will be capitalized—that is, the interest will be added to the principal amount of your loan, and additional interest will be based upon the higher amount. This will increase the total amount you have to repay.

Generally, if you're a dependent undergraduate student, you can borrow up to:

* $2,625 for freshmen
* $3,500 for sophomores
* $5,500 for juniors or seniors

If you're an independent undergraduate student or a dependent student whose parents are unable to get a PLUS Loan, you can generally borrow up to:

* $6,625 for freshmen
* $7,500 for sophomores
* $10,500 for juniors or seniors

There are many borrowing limit categories to these loans, depending on whether you get an unsubsidized or subsidized loan, which year in school you're enrolled, how long your program of study is, and if you're independent or dependent. You can have both kinds of Stafford loans at the same time, but the total amount of money loaned at any given time cannot exceed $23,000. The interest rate varies, but should not exceed 8.25%. The rate for the 1998–1999 school year was 7.43%. An origination fee for a Stafford loan is approximately three or four percent of the loan, and the fee will be deducted from each loan disbursement you receive. There is a six-month grace period after graduation before you must start repaying the loan.

Federal Direct Student Loans
Federal direct student loans have basically the same terms as the federal Stafford student loans and the PLUS loans for parents. The main difference is that the U.S. Department of Education is the lender instead of a bank. One advantage of federal direct student loans is that they offer a variety of repayment terms, such as a fixed monthly payment for ten years or a variable monthly payment for up to 25 years that is based on a percentage of income. This is a relatively new program, so not all colleges participate.

REPAYING YOUR LOANS
Once you begin repaying your loan, try to make all payments on time to build up or maintain a good credit rating. Defaulting on your loan could cause you to:

* have trouble getting credit in the future
* no longer qualify for federal or state educational financial aid

- have holds placed on your college records
- have your wages garnished
- have future federal income tax refunds taken
- have your assets seized

If you can't make payments on time, contact your servicer immediately. You may be able to get into a graduated or income-sensitive/income contingent repayment plan, deferment, or forbearance. If you are unemployed when your payments become due, you may be able to receive an unemployment deferment. For many loans, you will have a maximum repayment period of 10 years (excluding periods of deferment and forbearance).

FINANCIAL AID QUESTIONS AND ANSWERS

Here are answers to the most frequently asked questions about student financial aid:

1. *I probably don't qualify for aid—should I apply for aid anyway?* Yes. Many students and families mistakenly think they don't qualify for aid and fail to apply. The FAFSA form is free—there's no good reason for not applying.
2. *Do I need to be admitted at a particular college or university before I can apply for financial aid?* No. You can apply for financial aid any time after January 1. However, to get the funds, you must be admitted and enrolled in school.
3. *Do I have to reapply for financial aid every year?* Yes, and if your financial circumstances change, you may get either more or less aid. After your first year you will receive a "Renewal Application" which contains preprinted information from the previous year's FAFSA. Renewal of your aid also depends on your making satisfactory progress toward a degree and achieving a minimum GPA.
4. *Are my parents responsible for my educational loans?* No. You and you alone are responsible, unless they endorse or co-sign your loan. Parents are, however, responsible for the federal PLUS loans.
5. *If I take a leave of absence from school, do I have to start repaying my loans?* Not immediately, but you will after the grace period. Generally, though, if you use your grace period up during your leave, you'll have to begin repayment immediately after graduation, *unless* you apply for an extension of the grace period *before* it's used up.
6. *Are federal work-study earnings taxable?* Yes, you must pay federal and state income tax, although you may be exempt from social security taxes if you are enrolled full time and work less than 20 hours a week.

FINANCIAL AID CHECKLIST

_____ Explore financial aid options as soon as possible after you've decided to begin a culinary arts training program.

_____ Complete and mail the FAFSA as soon as possible after January 1st.

_____ Complete and mail other applications by the deadlines.

_____ Find out what your school requires and what financial aid they offer.

_____ Gather loan application information and forms from your college financial aid office. Forward the certified loan application to a participating lender: bank, savings and loan institution, or credit union, if necessary.

_____ Carefully read all letters and notices from the school, the federal student aid processor, the need analysis service, and private scholarship organizations. Note whether financial aid will be sent before or after you are notified about admission, and how exactly you will receive the money.

_____ Report any changes in your financial resources or expenses to your financial aid office, so they can adjust your award accordingly.

_____ Re-apply each year.

Financial Aid Acronyms Key	
COA	Cost of Attendance
EFC	Expected Family Contribution
EFT	Electronic Funds Transfer
ESAR	Electronic Student Aid Report
ETS	Educational Testing Service
FAA	Financial Aid Administrator
FAF	Financial Aid Form
FAFSA	Free Application for Federal Student Aid
FAO	Financial Aid Office
FDSLP	Federal Direct Student Loan Program
FFELP	Federal Family Education Loan Program
FSEOG	Federal Supplemental Educational Opportunity Grant
FWS	Federal Work-Study
GSL	Guaranteed Student Loan
PC	Parent Contribution
PLUS	Parent Loan for Undergraduate Students
SAP	Satisfactory Academic Progress
SC	Student Contribution
SLS	Supplemental Loan for Students

GLOSSARY OF FINANCIAL AID TERMS

Accrued interest: Interest that accumulates on the unpaid principal balance of your loan.

Capitalization of interest: Addition of accrued interest to the principal balance of your loan which increases both your total debt and monthly payments.

Default: Failure to repay your education loan.

Deferment: A period when a borrower, who meets certain criteria, may suspend loan payments.

Delinquency: Failure to make payments when due.

Disbursement: Loan funds issued by the lender.

Forbearance: Temporary adjustment to repayment schedule for cases of financial hardship.

Grace period: Specified period of time after you graduate or leave school during which you need not make payments.

Holder: The institution that currently owns your loan.

In-school grace, and **deferment interest subsidy:** Interest the federal government pays for borrowers on some loans while the borrower is in school, and during authorized deferments and grace periods.

Interest: Cost you pay to borrow money.

Interest-only payment: A payment that covers only interest owed on the loan and none of the principal balance.

Lender (Originator): Puts up the money when you take out a loan. Most lenders are financial institutions, but some state agencies and schools make loans too.

Origination fee: Fee, deducted from the principal, that is paid to the federal government to offset its cost of the subsidy to borrowers under certain loan programs.

Principal: Amount you borrow, which may increase as a result of capitalization of interest, and the amount on which you pay interest.

Promissory note: Contract between you and the lender that includes all the terms and conditions under which you promise to repay your loan.

Secondary markets: Institutions that buy student loans from originating lenders, thus providing lenders with funds to make new loans.

Servicer: Organization that administers and collects your loan. May be either the holder of your loan or an agent acting on behalf of the holder.

FINANCIAL AID RESOURCES

Here are several additional resources that you can use to obtain more information about financial aid.

Telephone Numbers

One or more of these phone numbers may prove helpful during the financial aid process.

Federal Student Aid Information Center (U.S. Department of Education)

Hotline 800-4-FED-AID (800-433-3243)

TDD Number for Hearing-Impaired 800-730-8913

For suspicion of fraud or abuse of federal aid ..800-MIS-USED (800-647-8733)

Selective Service..847-688-6888

Immigration and Naturalization (INS) 415-705-4205

Internal Revenue Service (IRS) 800-829-1040

Social Security Administration..800-772-1213

National Merit Scholarship Corporation 708-866-5100

Sallie Mae's College AnswerSM Service 800-222-7183

Career College Association 202-336-6828

Need Access/Need Analysis Service..800-282-1550

FAFSA on the WEB Processing/Software Problems.............................800-801-0576

Web Sites

Check out these Web sites for information about financial aid.

www.ed.gov/prog_info/SFAStudentGuide

The *Student Guide* is a free informative brochure about financial aid and is available on-line at the Department of Education's Web address listed here.

http://www.ed.gov/offices/OPE/express.html

This site enables you to fill out and submit the FAFSA on-line. You'll need to print out, sign, and send in the release and signature pages.

http://www.finaid.org/finaid

This site is called the Financial Aid Information Page. It lists a wealth of links to all types of financial aid information. Be sure to check it out.

http://www.career.org

This is the Web site of the Career College Association (CCA). It offers a limited number of scholarships for approximately 500 private post-secondary schools. The Web site gives you information about their scholarships and how you can apply for them.

http://www.salliemae.com

This Web site for Sallie Mae contains information about student loan programs. Also included are a helpful financial aid calculator and links to other financial aid Web pages.

http://www.fastweb.com

This site is called FastWEB.com. If you answer a few simple questions for them (such as name and address, geographic location, organizations that you are affiliated with, age, and so on), they will give you a free list of scholarships you might qualify for. Their database is updated regularly, and your list gets updated when new scholarships are added that fit your profile. FastWEB boasts that their database includes more than 400,000 awards.

http://www.advocacy-net.com/scholarmks.htm

Many helpful financial aid Web sites have links from this page, including the ever-popular ones mentioned above: fastweb and finaid. You can select a link to view a new Web page while the original page is still loading.

http://www.easi.ed.gov

This site is sponsored by the U. S. Department of Education, and it offers information about financial aid.

http://www.educaid.com

Educaid's Web site offers significant information about student loans and other forms of financial aid. They are student loan specialists.

Pamphlets

These two pamphlets are provided free of charge and offer a good overview of the financial aid process.

The Student Guide

Published by the U.S. Department of Education, this is the handbook about federal aid programs. To get a printed copy, call 1-800-4-FED-AID.

Looking for Student Aid

Published by the U.S. Department of Education, this is an overview of sources of information about financial aid. To get a printed copy, call 1-800-4-FED-AID.

Books

Take a look at any of the following books to get more information about the financial aid process.

Bear, John and Mariah Bear. *Bear's Guide to Finding Money for College 1998-1999.* Ten Speed Press, 1998.

Chany, Kalman. *Paying for College Without Going Broke, 1998 Edition.* The Princeton Review, 1998.

Davis, Herm and Joyce Kennedy. *College Financial Aid for Dummies.* IDG Books Worldwide, 1997.

Leider, Robert and Ann Leider. *Don't Miss Out: the Ambitious Student's Guide to Financial Aid.* Octameron, 1999.

Peterson's College Money Handbook 1999, 16th Edition. Peterson's, 1998.

Schlachter, Gail Ann. *1997-1999 Directory of Financial Aid for Women.* Reference Service Press.

The Scholarship Handbook 1999, 2nd Edition. The College Board, 1998.

Van Dusen, William and Bart Astor. *10 Minute Guide to Paying for College.* Arco Publishing, 1996.

Free Application for Federal Student Aid

1998–99 School Year

WARNING: If you purposely give false or misleading information on this form, you may be fined $10,000, sent to prison, or both.

"You" and "your" on this form always mean the student who wants aid.

Form Approved
OMB No. 1840-0110
App. Exp. 6/30/99

U.S. Department of Education
Student Financial
Assistance Programs

Use black ink or #2 pencil. Make capital letters and numbers clear and legible.

`E X M 9 6`

Fill in ovals completely. Only one oval per question. ● Correct

Incorrect marks may cause errors. Incorrect ✗ ✓

Section A: You (the student)

1–3. Your name

Your title (optional)

1. Last name   2. First name   3. M.I.

Mr. ○ 1   Miss, Mrs., or Ms. ○ 2

4–7. Your permanent mailing address
(All mail will be sent to this address. See Instructions, page 2 for state/country abbreviations.)

4. Number and street (Include apt. no.)

5. City   6. State   7. ZIP code

8. Your social security number (SSN) *(Don't leave blank. See Instructions, page 2.)*

9. Your date of birth

Month   Day   Year

`1 9`

10. Your permanent home telephone number

Area code

11. Your state of legal residence

State

12. Date you became a legal resident of the state in question 11 *(See Instructions, page 2.)*

Month   Year

`1 9`

13. Your driver's license number. *(If you don't have a license, write in "None.")*

License number

14. State that issued your driver's license.

State

15–16. Are you a U.S. citizen? *(See Instructions, pages 2–3.)*

Yes, I am a U.S. citizen. ○ 1

No, but I am an eligible noncitizen. ○ 2

A `⎕⎕⎕⎕⎕⎕⎕⎕`

No, neither of the above. ○ 3

17. As of today, are you married? *(Fill in only one oval.)*

I am not married. (I am single, widowed, or divorced.) ○ 1

I am married. ○ 2

I am separated from my spouse. ○ 3

18. Date you were married, separated, divorced, or widowed. If divorced, use date of divorce or separation, whichever is earlier.
(If never married, leave blank.) Month   Year

`1 9`

19. Will you have your first bachelor's degree before July 1, 1998? *(See Instructions, page 3.)*

Yes ○ 1
No ○ 2

20. Will you have received a high school diploma or earned a GED before the first date of your enrollment in college?

Yes ○ 1
No ○ 2

21. Highest educational level your father completed.

elementary school (K–8) ○ 1
high school (9–12) ○ 2
college or beyond ○ 3
unknown ○ 4

22. Highest educational level your mother completed.

elementary school (K–8) ○ 1
high school (9–12) ○ 2
college or beyond ○ 3
unknown ○ 4

If you (and your family) have **unusual circumstances**, complete this form and then check with your financial aid administrator. Examples:

- tuition expenses at an elementary or secondary school,
- unusual medical or dental expenses not covered by insurance,
- a family member who recently became unemployed, or
- other unusual circumstances such as changes in income or assets that might affect your eligibility for student financial aid.

Section B: Your Plans *Answer these questions about your college plans.*

23–27. Your expected enrollment status for the 1998–99 school year
(See Instructions, page 3.)

School term	Full time	3/4 time	1/2 time	Less than 1/2 time	Not enrolled
23. Summer term '98	○ 1	○ 2	○ 3	○ 4	○ 5
24. Fall semester/qtr. '98	○ 1	○ 2	○ 3	○ 4	○ 5
25. Winter quarter '98-99	○ 1	○ 2	○ 3	○ 4	○ 5
26. Spring semester/qtr. '99	○ 1	○ 2	○ 3	○ 4	○ 5
27. Summer term '99	○ 1	○ 2	○ 3	○ 4	○ 5

28. Your course of study *(See Instructions for code, page 3.)* **Code** ☐☐

29. College degree/certificate you expect to receive *(See Instructions for code, page 3.)* ☐

30. Date you expect to receive your degree/certificate Month ☐☐ Year ☐☐

31. Your grade level during the 1998–99 school year *(Fill in only one.)*

1st yr./never attended college ○ 1	5th year/other undergraduate ○ 6
1st yr./attended college before ○ 2	1st year graduate/professional ○ 7
2nd year/sophomore ○ 3	2nd year graduate/professional ○ 8
3rd year/junior ○ 4	3rd year graduate/professional ○ 9
4th year/senior ○ 5	Beyond 3rd year graduate/professional ○ 10

32–34. In addition to grants, what other types of financial aid are you (and your parents) interested in? *(See Instructions, page 3.)*

32. Student employment Yes ○ 1 No ○ 2

33. Student loans Yes ○ 1 No ○ 2

34. Parent loans for students Yes ○ 1 No ○ 2

35. If you are (or were) in college, do you plan to attend **that same college** in 1998–99? *(If this doesn't apply to you, leave blank.)* Yes ○ 1 No ○ 2

36–37. Veterans education benefits you expect to receive from July 1, 1998 through June 30, 1999

36. Amount per month $ ☐☐☐ .00

37. Number of months ☐☐

Section C: Student Status

38. Were you born **before** January 1, 1975? .... Yes ○ 1 No ○ 2

39. Are you a veteran of the U.S. Armed Forces? .... Yes ○ 1 No ○ 2

40. Will you be enrolled in a graduate or professional program (beyond a bachelor's degree) in 1998-99? .... Yes ○ 1 No ○ 2

41. Are you married? .... Yes ○ 1 No ○ 2

42. Are you an orphan or a ward of the court, or **were** you a ward of the court until age 18? .... Yes ○ 1 No ○ 2

43. Do you have legal dependents (**other than a spouse**) that fit the definition in Instructions, page 4? .... Yes ○ 1 No ○ 2

If you answered "Yes" to **any** question in Section C, go to Section D and fill out **only the STUDENT areas (WHITE areas)** on the rest of this form.

If you answered "No" to **every** question in Section C, go to Section D and fill out **both the STUDENT areas (WHITE areas) and the PARENTS areas (GRAY areas)** on the rest of this form.

Section D: Household Information

Remember:
At least one "Yes" answer in Section C means fill out the STUDENT areas (WHITE areas).

All "No" answers in Section C means fill out BOTH the STUDENT areas (WHITE areas) and the PARENTS areas (GRAY areas)..

STUDENT (& SPOUSE)

44. Number in your household in 1998–99 *(Include yourself and your spouse. Do not include your children and other people unless they meet the definition in Instructions, page 4.)* ☐☐

45. Number of college students in household in 1998–99 *(Of the number in 44, how many will be in college at least half-time in at least one term in an eligible program? Include yourself. See Instructions, page 4.)* ☐

PARENT(S) - GRAY area

46. Your parent(s)' **current** marital status:

single ○ 1   separated ○ 3   widowed ○ 5

married ○ 2   divorced ○ 4

47. Your parent(s)' state of legal residence State ☐☐

48. Date your parent(s) became legal resident(s) of the state in question 47 *(See Instructions, page 5.)* Month ☐☐ Year 1 9

49. Number in your parent(s)' household in 1998–99 *(Include yourself and your parents. Do not include your parent(s)' other children and other people unless they meet the definition in Instructions, page 5.)* ☐☐

50. Number of college students in household in 1998–99 *(Of the number in 49, how many will be in college at least half-time in at least one term in an eligible program? Include yourself. See Instructions, page 5.)* ☐

Section E: 1997 Income, Earnings, and Benefits *You must see Instructions, pages 5 and 6, for information about*   *Page 3*
tax forms and tax filing status, especially if you are estimating taxes or filing electronically or by telephone. These instructions will tell you what income and benefits should be reported in this section.

STUDENT (& SPOUSE)   **PARENT(S) - GRAY area**

The following 1997 U.S. income tax figures are from:

Everyone must fill out this column.
51. *(Fill in one oval.)*   **63.** *(Fill in one oval.)*

A—a completed 1997 IRS Form 1040A, 1040EZ, or 1040TEL .... ○ 1   A .... ○ 1

B—a completed 1997 IRS Form 1040 .... ○ 2   B .... ○ 2

C—an estimated 1997 IRS Form 1040A, 1040EZ, or 1040TEL .... ○ 3   C .... ○ 3

D—an estimated 1997 IRS Form 1040 .... ○ 4   D .... ○ 4

E—will not file a 1997 U.S. income tax return .... *(Skip to question 55.)* ○ 5   E *(Skip to 67.)* ○ 5

1997 Total number of exemptions (Form 1040–line 6d, or 1040A–line 6d; 1040EZ filers— *see Instructions, page 6.*)   **52.**   **64.**

1997 Adjusted Gross Income (AGI: Form 1040–line 32, 1040A–line 16, or 1040EZ–line 4—*see Instructions, page 6.*)   **53.** $ .00   **65.** $ .00

1997 U.S. income tax paid (Form 1040–line 46, 1040A–line 25, or 1040EZ–line 10.)   **54.** $ .00   **66.** $ .00

TAX FILERS ONLY

1997 Income earned from work   (Student) **55.** $ .00   (Father) **67.** $ .00

1997 Income earned from work   (Spouse) **56.** $ .00   (Mother) **68.** $ .00

1997 Untaxed income and benefits (yearly totals only):

Earned Income Credit (Form 1040–line 56a, Form 1040A–line 29c, or Form 1040EZ–line 8a)   **57.** $ .00   **69.** $ .00

Untaxed Social Security Benefits   **58.** $ .00   **70.** $ .00

AFDC/ADC or TANF *(See Instructions, pages 6 and 7.)*   **59.** $ .00   **71.** $ .00

Child support received for all children   **60.** $ .00   **72.** $ .00

Other untaxed income and benefits from Worksheet #2, page 11   **61.** $ .00   **73.** $ .00

1997 Amount from Line 5, Worksheet #3, page 12 *(See Instructions.)*   **62.** $ .00   **74.** $ .00

Section F: Asset Information   **ATTENTION!**

Fill out Worksheet A or Worksheet B in Instructions, page 7. *If you meet the tax filing and income conditions on Worksheets A and B, you do not have to complete Section F to apply for Federal student aid. Some states and colleges, however, require Section F information for their own aid programs. Check with your financial aid administrator and/or State Agency.*

Age of your older parent   **82.**

STUDENT (& SPOUSE)   **PARENT(S) - GRAY area**

Cash, savings, and checking accounts   **75.** $ .00   **83.** $ .00

Other real estate and investments value *(Don't include the home.)*   **76.** $ .00   **84.** $ .00

Other real estate and investments debt *(Don't include the home.)*   **77.** $ .00   **85.** $ .00

Business value   **78.** $ .00   **86.** $ .00

Business debt   **79.** $ .00   **87.** $ .00

Investment farm value *(See Instructions, page 8.)* *(Don't include a family farm.)*   **80.** $ .00   **88.** $ .00

Investment farm debt *(See Instructions, page 8.)* *(Don't include a family farm.)*   **81.** $ .00   **89.** $ .00

Section G: Releases and Signatures

90–101. What college(s) do you plan to attend in 1998–99?
(Note: The colleges you list below will have access to your application information. See Instructions, page 8.)

Housing codes	1—on-campus	3—with parent(s)
	2—off-campus	

	Title IV School Code	OR	College Name	College Street Address and City	State	Housing Code
XX.	0 5 4 3 2 1		EXAMPLE UNIVERSITY	14930 NORTH SOMEWHERE BLVD. ANYWHERE CITY	S T	XX. 2
90.						91.
92.						93.
94.						95.
96.						97.
98.						99.
100.						101.

102. The U.S. Department of Education will send information from this form to your state financial aid agency and the state agencies of the colleges listed above so they can consider you for state aid. Answer **"No"** if you **don't** want information released to the state. *(See Instructions, page 9 and "Deadlines for State Student Aid," page 10.)* .... 102. No ○ 2

103. Males not yet registered for Selective Service (SS). Do you want SS to register you? *(See Instructions, page 9.)* .... 103. Yes ○ 1

104–105. Read, Sign, and Date Below

By signing below, you certify that all the information on this form is true and complete to the best of your knowledge. If asked, you agree to give proof of the information, which may include a copy of your U.S. or state income tax form. If you purposely give false or misleading information, you may be fined $10,000, sent to prison, or both. You also certify that:

- you will use any federal student aid funds received during the award year covered by this application solely for educational expenses related to attendance during that year at the institution of higher education that determined eligibility for those funds;
- you are not in default on a Title IV educational loan, or you have repaid or made satisfactory arrangements to repay your loan if you are in default;
- you do not owe an overpayment on a Title IV educational grant, or you have made satisfactory arrangements to repay that overpayment; and
- you will notify your school if you do owe an overpayment or are in default.

Everyone whose information is given on this form should sign below. The student (and at least one parent, if parental information is given) must sign below or this form will be returned unprocessed.

104. Signatures *(Sign in the boxes below.)*

¹ Student

² Student's Spouse

³ Father/Stepfather

⁴ Mother/Stepmother

105. Date completed
Month Day Year
1998 ○
1999 ○

Section H: Preparer's Use Only

For preparers other than student, spouse, and parent(s). Student, spouse, and parent(s), sign in question 104.

Preparer's name (last, first, M.I.)

Firm name

Firm or preparer's address (street, city, state, ZIP)

106. Employer identification number (EIN)
OR

107. Preparer's social security number

108. Certification: All of the information on this form is true and complete to the best of my knowledge.

¹ Preparer's Signature   Date

School Use Only
D/O ○¹   Title IV Code

¹ FAA Signature

MDE Use Only
Do not write in this box   Special handle

MAKE SURE THAT YOU HAVE COMPLETED, DATED, AND SIGNED THIS APPLICATION.
Mail the original application (NOT A PHOTOCOPY) to: Federal Student Aid Programs, P.O. Box 4001, Mt. Vernon, IL 62864-8601

Who:	Sharon Odmann
What:	Chef Owner of Kiyote Cowboy Cookery & Personal Chef Services
Where:	Lancaster, Pennsylvania
How long:	Four years in the culinary arts field

Insider's Advice

If you're interested in getting into the culinary arts, take some culinary courses, so you learn the basics. You can earn an associate degree in two years. Also, try to get hired on at a catering company. Caterers know the ins and outs of the business; they know how to make food beautiful. You can translate the experience to a restaurant kitchen later if you want. To succeed as a caterer, you need to be willing to work hard. You should also have great listening abilities so you can find out what your clients want, communication skills, and cheerfulness. People in food-service are often grumpy, and they often do a lot of screaming and hollering. You almost need to have a Teflon skin to not let that type of behavior affect you.

If you're working as a line cook and want to advance your career, focus on learning as much as you can. Learn about all of the facets of the back of the house. A good question to ask yourself is this: What else can you do to make this product better—what is one more thing you can do to give it a another subtle flavor and what is one more thing you can do to make it look nicer?

Insider's Take on the Future

The future direction of the culinary arts field can be summed up in two phrases: Home Meal Replacement (HMR) and Personal Chef Industry. Nobody's eating at home anymore. People are too busy—many work 10-hour days, then go pick up their kids and drive them places. Boston Market started the HMR phenomenon and now the grocery stores are jumping into it. People can walk into a grocery store, pick up a meal that's already cooked, and go home and eat it.

The iceberg hasn't even been scratched yet in HMR. The personal chef industry is an outreach of that. Personal chefs go into a home and cook meals for people. Many families want to have home-cooked food because they really miss it. So the personal chef industry will really take off. Restaurants will latch onto the

HMR industry too. More of them will start offering foods in a deli case, so people can swing by, choose a meal, and take it home.

Another piece of advice is to find a niche market within the foodservice industry. There are a lot of needs out there that aren't being met. You could serve food to people who have special dietary restrictions. For instance, patients who leave the hospital after kidney failure may be told by their dietitian not to eat potassium. Well, if you become an expert in potassium and how to cook without it, you could fill that niche market.

Another niche market is giving cooking classes to people in the privacy of their own homes. As more people become interested in cooking, this market will grow. You could build up a business from that.

CHAPTER | 5

In this chapter, you'll find out how to land a great culinary arts job. First, you'll get the inside scoop on how to conduct your job search from networking and researching the field to using on-line resources. Then, you'll find tips and techniques for writing resumes and cover letters and acing job interviews.

HOW TO LAND A GREAT JOB

Approach your job search with focus, determination, and a positive attitude, and you'll be sure to come out a winner. Many tools exist to help you land a great job in the culinary arts. Before you start gearing up for the job hunt, however, take some time to evaluate your interests, desires, and personal financial situation. Culinary educator and chef Geraldine Born gives this advice to her culinary students before they go out to look for a job. She says:

> Take a long look at yourself to understand what makes you happy. Do you enjoy following recipes? Would you mind doing that every day? If not, then perhaps working in a fran-

chise restaurant is for you. However, if you prefer something more creative, then you'll want to go where you'll have the chance to come up with new recipes—perhaps an independent restaurant that offers dinner specials or a mom and pop place that allows flexibility in menu planning. Or if you love garde manger, then look for a job with a banquet hall or a hotel that regularly hosts banquets. If you desire a good benefits package and moderate hours, you may look at jobs in institutional cooking. You need to know yourself and where your interests lie, so you can choose the position that is best for you.

Once you've focused in on an area of culinary arts that appeals to you, how do you go about getting a great job in that area? Read on to learn about the latest job hunting tools you can use to secure a culinary position that's right for you.

CONDUCTING YOUR JOB SEARCH

Using several different methods of job searching will increase your chances for success. For instance, don't rely exclusively on the Help Wanted advertisements in your local newspaper to find a job. If you take advantage of all the job hunting resources that are available today, you can locate and apply for jobs all over the country. One excellent resource you can use if you are in a culinary training program is the school's job placement office.

Your School's Job Placement Office

If you are attending a culinary school, or if you've graduated from one that offers lifetime job placement assistance, this should be your first stop on the job hunt. Many culinary schools provide a wide range of services to aid students in their job search. Visit the job placement office, ask some questions, and find out what your school's job placement rate of success is. It may calm your fears of landing a good job upon graduation. Some schools claim that 90%–100% of their graduates obtain jobs within six months of graduation. Other schools boast that their graduates get four or five different job offers to choose from. Ask what services the job placement office offers to students. You may be able to obtain personalized career counseling, participate in mock interviews, or attend a campus job fair. Ask a counselor in the placement office if he or she has a list of the alumni who are willing to network with students for job leads. Take advantage of as many services as you possibly can to increase your odds of landing your dream job.

Using Your Public Library

Go visit your local public library; it has a wealth of information available about the culinary arts industry. For example, many libraries carry periodicals that focus on the industry, such as *Bon Appetit, Gourmet,* or *Food and Wine.* You may want to browse through these magazines to locate restaurants or chefs you are interested in. Then, ask a librarian how to find the phone number or address of a particular restaurant discussed in one of the magazines—and you'll have a possible job lead. Call or write to the chef at the restaurant to inquire about possible job openings.

You can also ask a reference librarian where the library's *Career* section is located, so you can browse through books on job hunting and writing resumes. Be sure to look in both the circulating and reference collection. While you check out books in the circulating collection, the most recent and up-to-date books are often found only in the reference section. You normally can't check out reference books, but you can read them in the library. An example of a good reference book is the *Adams Job Almanac* (published in 1998 by the Adams Media Corporation). You can turn to the chapter entitled *Hotels, Restaurants, and Casinos* to find contact information and profiles of specific companies that are interested in hiring culinary arts professionals. Using your library's resources is a good way to collect information that will jump start your job search.

Sample Job Postings

These sample job postings can give you an idea of what type of requirements and pay levels are available. Of course, job duties, benefits, and salaries vary considerably, but these sample postings culled from a variety of sources can give you an idea of what's out there.

Position:	Culinary Arts Instructor for the federal government
Location:	Albuquerque, NM
Requirements:	Four-year college major in education, culinary arts, food science, dietetics, nutrition, food service management/hospitality, or a related science, plus one year of additional related experience.
Salary:	$31,897 per year

Position:	Sous Chef
Location:	Long Beach, California
Requirements:	Must be innovative and creative. One year's experience in similar position as sous chef. Must be ready to apply yourself. Culinary degree preferred.
Description:	New 100-seat upscale restaurant needs sous chef to create something special. Open for lunch and dinner, seven days a week. Two weeks paid vacation. Chance to work with a successful chef.
Salary:	$28,000–$32,000 annually

Position:	Pastry Chef
Location:	Vail, Colorado
Description:	Create and prepare all items for dessert menu. Prepare and display creative desserts for banquets, create birthday cakes, cookies, pies, etc. for a four-diamond property.
Requirements:	Knowledge of bake shop techniques required. Minimum of two years' pastry experience and culinary training preferred. Creativity and willingness to work flexible schedule is required.
Salary:	$11–$14 per hour, depending on experience. Excellent benefits package included.

Calling Job Hotlines

Many large corporations sponsor a job hotline, which is a recorded message that lists specific job openings with that corporation. The phone message is updated regularly with new jobs, and may be organized by subject area if the number of open jobs is substantial. You'll need a touch-tone phone to access a job hotline. You can check your local newspaper's classified ads for a listing of job-lines. Another resource is the book entitled *The 1997 National Job Hotline Directory* by Marcia Williams and Sue Cubbage. It is arranged by state, and within each state, by general job category. You can find a state in which you'd like to work and then look under the heading *Hospitality* for a list of companies and their job hotline telephone numbers. Most of the companies listed are hotels, such as Hilton, Embassy Suites, Doubletree, Marriott, Westin, and the Ritz Carlton, so if you're interested in working for a hotel restaurant, calling job hotlines could be a useful tool in your job search.

Job Searching on the Internet

One of the fastest growing resources for job hunters is the Internet. If you don't have your own computer, try to access one at your local public library or at school, if you are attending classes. Many professional associations host Web sites that include industry information and some also include job-related information. In addition, the federal government and several national private job banks have Web sites with thousands of job listings all over the country. Here are several on-line resources that post information about culinary arts jobs. All sites offer free information to job hunters, unless otherwise noted.

http://www.escoffier.com

This site, called Escoffier On Line (EOL), offers information about food service employment and education. The site includes a searchable *Help Wanted* section and a *Position Sought* section. It is not an employment agency, but it does offer free resources to people seeking executive chef, chef, pastry chef, baker, and line cook jobs, as well as hotel, resort, and cruise ship jobs. The site includes many links to other useful culinary Web sites, organized by subject category.

http://www.starchefs.com

The Star Chefs Web site includes a *Culinary Help Wanted* section that lists openings for jobs such as line cook, pastry cook, garde manger, oyster shucker, executive chef, sous chef, and more. The site includes information about celebrity chefs and prominent food experts, as well as recipes, tips, reviews, and trends.

http://www.hospitalitylink.com

This Web site, Hospitality Link, is focused on employment and staffing for the hospitality industry. You can click on *Culinary* to access nationwide job openings for chefs, pastry chefs, executive chefs, and sous chefs. The site also offers links to recruiters, employers, resume services, industry-related sites, and resume postings.

http://npe.aug.com/acf/jobbank.html

This site of the American Culinary Federation (ACF) contains a list of job openings around the country, ranging from cook to sous chef to executive chef. The ACF job bank posts job openings for 60 days, and the postings can be viewed by current ACF members or by nonmembers who pay a fee. The job bank will not only give you the opportunity to look at job openings in the culinary industry, but also will give prospective employers the chance to look at your resume. Resumes may be posted for one year by ACF members or by nonmembers who pay a fee, and they can be viewed by the general public.

http://www.coolworks.com
Coolworks provides links to over 60,000 job openings at camps, resorts, cruise ships, guest ranches, and more. Many of the jobs are in the hospitality and food service industry; some are seasonal and some are permanent. The job openings are organized by state or by job category, such as camp jobs, resort jobs, cruise ship jobs, and so on.

http://www.usajobs.opm.gov
If you are looking for a cooking job with the federal government, check out the Web site of the United States Office of Personnel Management. Click on *Current Job Openings* and then go to the index. When the index appears, click on the letter "C" to see a list of federal jobs for cooks, chefs, and cooking instructors.

http://www.careerpath.com
This site, Career Path, offers an on-line version of newspaper employment ads from over seventy cities in America. You can search by keyword or the job category *food service.* This site is helpful if you want to look for jobs in other parts of the country, but remember that you'll be competing with everyone who is reading the print version of that area's newspaper. Some of the newspapers featured include the *New York Times*, the *Washington Post*, and the *Miami Herald.* The site includes company profiles and career advice.

http://www.chat-network.com
This site is called the Casino, Hospitality, and Travel Network, and it includes employer profiles (alphabetical list or by state), job listings, and a resource room of links to several job-related Web sites.

http://www.hotel-online.com/Neo
This site is called Hotel Online, and it features several hospitality news stories, an on-line forum, and classified advertisements including employment opportunities and restaurants for sale. You can also perform a search of Hotel Online's hospitality article database.

http://www.nacufs.org

This is the site for The National Association of College & University Food Services (NACUFS), a trade association for food service professionals at over 600 institutions of higher education in the United States, Canada, and abroad. It includes a job bulletin with many open managerial positions at NACUFS schools such as chef, sous chef, executive chef, banquet manager, food service manager, catering manager, director, and more.

http://www.hospitality-pro.com

The Hospitality ProServices Web site provides information and job listings for people in the hospitality industry. You may want to visit this site on a regular basis since the jobs are updated regularly.

http://www.restaurantreport.com/Jobs/Index.html

This is a new feature on the Restaurant Report's Web site. It lists job openings such as sous chef, restaurant manager, and chef. It also includes links to hospitality recruitment companies.

http://www.kitchenette.com/jobs/index.html

This site, entitled Kitchenette, is an on-line magazine celebrating food in the San Francisco Bay area. It also lists job openings in the Bay area, so if you live in the area or are considering relocating to it, this site is a must to check out.

http://www.foodnet.com/

Food Net includes a section entitled *Help Wanted/Needed*, where you can find job openings or post a message describing your skills and the type of job you are looking for. It is a section of a forum called Food Talk, so the tone is informal. Other features included at this site are: writers' corner, food chat, food links, food news, and featured chefs.

http://www.renard-international.com

The Renard International Hospitality Consultants Web site offers information about the company, such as its mission, goals, and areas of specialization. It is a recruitment company—applicants do not pay fees to register with them. Their job openings include positions such as kitchen manager, executive chef, pastry chef, garde manger, and chef de partie.

http://careermosaic.com

Career Mosaic offers lists of job postings and company profiles for a variety of industries and hosts on-line job fairs. The site is not focused on culinary jobs, although it does list a few. You're more apt to find culinary jobs with large corporations or franchises at this site.

http://www.monster.com

The Monster Board posts a large number of job openings in a variety of fields and offers career tips to its visitors. You can search under the job category *Hospitality—Tourism—Chef* to locate chef, sous chef, and executive chef positions.

Classified Advertisements

If you are looking for a job in your local area, don't neglect to scan the classified ads in the newspaper. You may find a job that interests you, so take the time to read the entire section carefully. Large display ads may announce new restaurants that are looking for an entire kitchen staff before they open. Keep in mind that jobs may be listed under several different names and categories in the employment classified section, such as cook, line cook, chef, hospitality, restaurant, or kitchen. Here are a few samples of what you might find:

> SAUTÉ COOK: Experienced sauté cook starts at $10.00 an hour. Both full-time and part-time positions available in busy family restaurant. Start immediately.

> BAKER wanted for busy natural foods café. Must be experienced in baking from scratch. Call for an interview.

> NEW franchise restaurant opening. Broiler cooks, fry cooks, pantry cooks, and sauté cooks wanted. Fun work environment plus health, life, and dental benefits, as well as a 401K plan.

GETTING A HEALTH CERTIFICATE

Health certificates for foodhandlers and foodservice managers are mandated by jurisdictions in each county, city, or state. Therefore, you should be aware of the laws in the area in which you are seeking employment. You can find this information by calling the local department of health—you can find the number by looking in the phone book or on the Internet. Or you can access the Educational Foundation of the National Restaurant Association's Web site, which lists local jurisdiction requirements broken down by state: http://www.edfound.org/servsafe.htm.

The guidelines for obtaining a health certificate and how to do it vary among counties, cities, and states. For example, in Apache County in Arizona, all food-handlers should have a Foodhandler Card, which is obtained by attending a free health department class. In another county in Arizona, La Paz, all foodhandlers must have a County Health card. Applicants for the card must watch a 17-minute video, pass a 20-question exam, and pay a $10 fee. In Corpus Christi, Texas, all foodhandlers must have foodhandler certification. They can obtain this by attending a two-hour course at the health department or by taking a ServSafe course (described below), which is offered at a local college. Many jurisdictions do not require cooks or chefs to have heath certificates or foodhandler cards if there is a certified foodservice manager on the premises. Fees required for obtaining a health certificate vary widely, from free to over $50.

A national food safety training program called ServSafe is sponsored by the Educational Foundation of the National Restaurant Association. If you enroll in and pass this certification process, you'll be granted a ServSafe certificate that is accepted in 95% of the jurisdictions across the nation. ServSafe courses may be offered by a culinary school, the local health department, or directly from the Educational Foundation of the National Restaurant Association (their contact information is in Appendix A).

Many culinary schools include a course or seminar on food safety and sani-tation, in which you earn your area's health certificate or a ServSafe certificate. If you earn a local health certificate and then move to work in a different area, you'll need to find out if the new location will honor it. Again, contact the local health department for the answer. Getting all this information may seem daunting, but it is just one more step in a successful job search.

The Jobs Are Out There

Several thousand new positions will become available every year since kitchen jobs will increase faster than the average of all occupations through the year 2006.

According to the Bureau of Labor Statistics

NETWORKING

Networking has become a major job search tactic used by people in all industries. Essentially, it is just talking to people you already know or meeting new people to talk about some aspect of the culinary arts. For instance, you can network with your friends, relatives, and acquaintances to find out if they know of a restaurant that is hiring or of an experienced chef in your area who would be an excellent mentor. And you can network with other cooks and chefs to find out if they like where they work. Once you land a job, you will probably be networking with your coworkers to find out more information about various specialties in the culinary arts field, such as pastry arts, garde manager, meat cutting, and others.

You can add to your network when you visit various kitchens looking for employment. While most cooks and chefs are very busy, they often will take a few minutes out of their day to talk to a newcomer to the field. They were beginners once themselves, so if you are careful not to take up too much of their time, they may give you some useful information. Here are some typical questions you can ask cooks about their jobs:

- How do you like working here?
- What are the benefits of working here?
- What is the kitchen atmosphere like?
- How does the executive chef treat you?
- Where else have you worked, and how does this place compare?

You can gather a lot of information in a casual way, just by talking to as many people as you can. When you leave each kitchen or restaurant, jot down some notes on what you heard and learned, so you can organize the information and access it later. After you talk to a lot of people in different kitchens, you may start forgetting what each person had to say.

Networking with other culinary arts professionals can also give you inside information on local or regional trends. You can find out what other chefs are doing and which restaurants are hiring. You may also get the scoop on which chefs are planning to expand their kitchens to include pastry chefs or additional workers. Then you can add those kitchens to your list of places to visit.

Maintaining Your Contacts

It is important to maintain your contacts once you have established them. Try to contact people again within a couple of weeks of meeting them. You can always ask a question, send a piece of information related to your conversation, or just send a note of thanks. This contact will cement your meeting in their minds, so they will remember you more readily when you get in touch in the future. If you haven't communicated with your contacts for a few months, you might send them a note or e-mail about an article you read, a special culinary technique, or relevant new culinary tool just to keep your name fresh in their minds.

Contacting Chefs

After you've narrowed your list down to three or four chefs for whom you would like to work, the next hurdle is to gain an interview. You should find out the schedule of each chef before trying to make contact. Once you know a convenient time to call, call the chefs and tell them that you're interested in working for them. Ask if there are currently any openings and if so, request an interview. Even if there aren't any openings in their kitchen, ask if you can come in to observe or work in the kitchen for a few days for free. That way, you can gather more information, make a good impression, and find out if you can apply after gaining more experience. When you visit each chef's kitchen, bring a few copies of your resume with you.

Culinary Scoop

What is a gastronome? A *gastronome* is a person who enjoys and has a discriminating taste for foods.

WRITING YOUR RESUME

A resume gives prospective employers a written history of your skills, knowledge, and work experience at a glance. While many entry-level culinary jobs do not require a resume, you will impress prospective employers if you bring one to your interview. Even if it is only stapled to your application form, a well-written resume will help sell your talents and make you stand out from the crowd. As you gain experience and education, the importance of having a resume will grow; if you are applying for a job as a sous chef, chef, or executive chef, you'll definitely need to have one. Your resume should summarize your employment history and your qualifications for the job you're seeking. While there are many different formats for resumes, all resumes should contain the following information:

+ name, address, telephone number (and e-mail address if applicable)
+ employment objective—the type of work or specific job you're looking for
+ work experience—job title, name of employer, and usually the dates of employment (including part time and volunteer)
+ description of duties you performed on your previous job(s)
+ education, including school name, highest grade completed, and type of certification, diploma, or degree awarded
+ special skills, proficiency in foreign languages, and honors or awards
+ membership in professional organizations or associations
+ professional qualifications or certifications

How to Organize Your Resume

There are many ways of organizing a resume, but the three most common are:

+ the chronological format
+ the functional (or skills) format
+ the combination format

In the first, you list the dates of your past employment in chronological order. This is a good format for people who have continuous work experience with little or no breaks in between jobs. However, the functional format is good for people who have been absent from the workforce or who have large gaps in employment. In the functional format, you emphasize the skills or qualifications that you have and not the dates of employment. The combination format combines aspects of both the chronological and functional formats.

Choose the format that best highlights your training, experience, and expertise. Take a look at the sample resumes appearing on the next few pages to get ideas for creating your own resume. Other examples can be found in publications available from your public library or local bookstore (see Appendix B for books about resumes).

The length and variety of your work experience is your best guide to your resume's length, but one page is generally preferred for a standard resume, and never longer than two. When you've finished writing your resume, ask someone you trust to read it and suggest ways to improve it.

Resume Tips and Techniques

Here are a few additional suggestions for preparing your resume:

- Use standard letter size ivory, cream, or neutral-colored paper. Smaller resumes may get thrown out or lost and larger ones will get crumpled edges.
- Emphasize your name by either making it larger than anything else on the page, or by making it bold or italic, or some combination thereof.
- Use a font that is easy to read, such as 12-point Times New Roman.
- Prepare several different resumes, emphasizing the specific culinary skills needed for each job you are applying for.
- Be honest when describing your job experience and qualifications.
- Use bullet points and short phrases instead of long sentences.
- Do not include personal information on your resume such as your birth date, race, marital status, or religion.
- Do not crowd your resume—shorten the margins if you need more space.
- Use action words, such as managed, conducted, developed, or produced.
- Be consistent when using bold, capitalization, underlining, and italics. If one company name is underlined, make sure all are underlined. Check titles and dates too.
- Keep your resume updated. Don't write "1/99 to Present," if you ended your job two months ago. People perceive that as misrepresentation.
- Include your name, address, and phone number on every page (if longer than one page).
- Do not cross out anything or handwrite any comments on your resume.
- Proofread your final draft very carefully. Read it backward and forward. Have your friends with good proofreading skills read it, too.

References

Employers interested in hiring you may want speak to people who can accurately describe your work experience and personal qualities—that is, your references. How do you come up with references? Well, the first step is to create a list of former supervisors, teachers, or other professionals with whom you have interacted. You want to select people who know you well and who would heartily recommend you to an employer. However, be aware that it's standard practice not to include any relatives as references. Before you narrow down your list to three or four people, contact each person to ask for permission to list him or her as a reference.

You can include a list of your references with each resume you give out, or you can simply state at the bottom of the resume that you have references available. If you are responding to an advertisement, read it carefully to see if you are supposed to send references. If the ad does not mention them, you probably don't need to send them with your resume. List your references on a separate sheet of paper, and remember to include your name, address, and phone number at the top of the list. For each reference that you list, provide the following information:

- name
- address
- telephone number
- job title

You may not need to provide a separate list of references, but it's handy to carry such a list along to job interviews. If you are asked to complete a job application, then you can easily fill in the information about each reference.

Sample Chronological Resume

MIGUEL T. GOMEZ, CC
242 West Palm Beach Avenue
Palm Beach, FL 33765
813-441-1112

OBJECTIVE

Lead Line Cook

EXPERIENCE

1996-Present
Maria's Trattoria
West Palm Beach, Florida
Line Cook
Grill and sauté stations
Create dinner specials twice a week
Prepare soups and sauces daily
Volume restaurant, with 1,500+ covers per week

1994-1996
Celeste's Cafe
Ft. Lauderdale, Florida
Prep Cook
Prepared daily mise en place for various stations
Assisted cooks at pantry, grill, and sauté stations

EDUCATION

Diploma in Culinary Arts from the Pinellas Technical Education Center. St. Petersburg, Florida, 1996.

Diploma. Countryside High School. Palm Harbor, Florida, 1994.

QUALIFICATIONS AND SKILLS

- American Culinary Federation Certified Culinarian
- ServSafe Sanitation certified by National Restaurant Association
- Fluent in Spanish
- References provided upon request

Sample Functional Resume

Madeleine LeTourneau, CSC

476 Sunnyside Drive ✦ San Jose, CA 94302 ✦ 415-784-2358

Objective: Sous Chef or Chef de Cuisine

Qualifications

Two years of experience as a sous chef

American Culinary Federation Certified Sous Chef

Four years of experience as a line cook

Two years training and supervising line cooks

Banquet and garde manger experience

Professional Experience

Prepared daily a variety of quality soups and sauces from scratch

Planned and cooked daily menu specials

Managed six line cooks, including hiring and firing as needed

Assisted executive chef in daily operation of kitchen

Skilled at containing food costs

Maintained ingredient inventory system

Employment History

Sous Chef, A Touch of France, 1996-Present

Lead Cook and banquet work, Holiday Sun Resort, 1994-1996

Line Cook, Waterfront View, 1993-1994

Grill and Fry Cook, Tangy Tuesday's, 1992-1993

Pantry Cook, Sweetwater's, 1991-1992

Garde manger and banquet assistant, Hilton Resort, 1990-1991

Education

A. O. S. Degree in Culinary Arts from the California Culinary Academy, San Francisco, 1996.

Award

ACF Food Salon Silver Medal Winner, Junior Chef Competition, 1995.

Sample Combination Resume

LAWRENCE BING
320 Oak Grove Boulevard
Brooklyn, NY 10015
718-425-6842

Objective: Pastry Chef / Baker

SUMMARY OF QUALIFICATIONS

One and a half years experience as pastry chef for prestigious country club

Mixed and baked cookies; formed and baked specialty breads for high-volume bakery

Baked, prepared, and decorated cakes and pastries using creative techniques

Prepared desserts for banquets and events for up to 500 guests

PROFESSIONAL EXPERIENCE

Pastry Chef, River Heights Golf and Country Club

Long Island, NY, 1997-Present

Responsible for production of all baked goods for clubhouse banquets, including breads, desserts, and specialty items.

Baker, Larry's Bakeshop & Cafe

Brooklyn, NY, 1995-1997

Head baker of retail bakery; baked and decorated cookies, breads, pies, and cakes.

Pastry Chef Assistant, The Verazzano Hotel

Brooklyn, NY, 1994-1995

Assisted the pastry chef in all aspects of bakery production for the hotel's restaurant and room service. Helped bake and prepare specialty items for banquets.

EDUCATION

A. A. S., Baking and Pastry Arts. Johnson & Wales University, Providence RI, 1995.

B. A., English. New York University, New York, NY, 1993.

WRITING A COVER LETTER

Once you've got your resume looking perfect, it's time to concentrate on your cover letter. A cover letter is a way to introduce yourself to prospective employers. It should be brief and capture the employer's attention, and it should not repeat too much of what is in the resume. Follow a business letter format, and include the following information:

- the name and address of the specific person to whom the letter is addressed
- the name of the job you are applying for
- the reason for your interest in the company or position
- your main qualifications for the position (in brief)
- a request for an interview
- your phone number and address

A hiring manager may have several job openings at one time, so you should clearly describe which job you are applying for. If you are responding to an advertisement in the newspaper or on the Internet, make sure you state the exact job title that's in the ad. Many human resources departments track the success of their ads, so include the source where you saw the position advertised.

Take the time to do some investigating, so you can address your cover letter to someone specific, if possible. Call the company and ask for the hiring manager's or human resources representative's name. If it is the company's policy not to give out names, at least get the person's formal title and use that in place of a person's name.

In the body of your cover letter, think of a way to summarize your qualifications effectively. You obviously don't have room to list the details of all the jobs you have held, so try to come up with a succinct summary, such as "I have three years' experience as a sauté cook and two years' experience in garde manger." You can draw attention to the most important parts of your work experience, but don't get bogged down in repeating everything that's in your resume. Show enthusiasm for the job in your cover letter and express your desire for obtaining an interview in a clear, straightforward manner.

Sample Cover Letter

Miguel T. Gomez
242 West Palm Beach Avenue
Palm Beach, FL 33765
813-441-1112

March 10, 1999

Ms. Stephani Jones
Executive Chef
Café European
451 Beach Tree Lane
West Palm Beach, FL 33745

Dear Chef Jones:

It is with great interest that I read your advertisement on the Escoffier On-Line Internet Web site for a Lead Line Cook.

As you can see from my enclosed resume, I have headed the grill and sauté stations at Maria's Trattoria for two years. While in this position, I have become certified as a culinarian by the American Culinary Federation. I am experienced in planning and cooking dinner specials on a regular basis, and have been greatly praised by the executive chef and our customers for the creativity of my plate presentations. I have volunteered to manage the other line cooks and have done so on four separate occasions with outstanding results. My culinary skills, creativity, and teamwork ability make me an excellent candidate for this position.

Should you agree that my qualifications are a good match for your needs, please call me at 813-441-1112. I look forward to meeting you. Thank you in advance for your time and consideration.

Sincerely,

Miguel T. Gomez

Resume Enclosed

ACING YOUR INTERVIEW

During the course of your culinary career, you'll probably go on several job interviews.

So it makes sense to spend some time going over interview basics, such as what to wear, how to answer and ask questions, and essentially how to make a great impression.

Personal Appearance

While there is some flexibility in the dress code for culinary arts professionals who are job hunting, it's safe to assume that you should present yourself professionally for every interview. Exactly how you dress will depend on the type and level of the job you are seeking. For instance, experienced chefs may go on an interview dressed in their kitchen uniform, commonly known as their *whites*. However, a line cook may dress neatly in casual but clean and ironed pants and shirt. While you won't often need to wear a corporate suit to an interview, you should strive to project a professional appearance.

Interview Tips

- Show enthusiasm and genuine interest in the position.
- Arrive early or exactly on time—before the day of the interview, visit your destination, so you know where to go.
- If you're asked about a skill you don't possess, admit it, but say you're willing to learn.
- Use standard formal English and avoid slang.
- Thank the interviewer at the completion of the interview.

What to Do During the Interview

One of the most important things you can do during an interview is to relax and just *be yourself.* Often, an executive chef or other manager will say they hired someone just because they felt a connection with that person. Perhaps it was a gut feeling, or just a sense that this person would fit into their team. If you act stiff and uptight, the interviewer may not be able to see the real you and won't get that inner sense that you are the best person for the job.

Greet your interviewer with a firm handshake and make eye contact during the greeting. This is no time to be shy or timid. Focus on speaking confidently throughout the interview and answer questions in complete sentences, not just *yes* or *no*. However, don't ramble on too long answering any one question. A good rule of thumb is to keep your answers under two to three minutes each. Prepare carefully for each interview—learn as much as you can about the restaurant or establishment before the interview. It will help you sound knowledgeable when answering and asking questions during the interview.

Answering Questions

It's a good idea to practice asking and answering sample interview questions with a friend or relative to brush up on your presentation and communication skills. Here are some of the most common interview questions along with tips on how to answer them.

Tell me about yourself.

Begin your answer with a short prepared statement that focuses on your training, qualifications, or work experience. You don't need to provide any personal information in your answer about your marital status, religion, age, or hobbies. For example:

> I am a hard-working cook dedicated to professional growth and excellence, with four years of experience on the line, working the pantry, pasta, and grill stations.

What are your strengths and weaknesses?

You can launch directly into your "best" strength and discuss it at length. Then briefly describe a weakness, followed by another strength. This way you sandwich a negative in between two positives. Whatever you do, don't spend more time talking about your weaknesses than you do about your strengths.

It may help to list your strengths and weaknesses on a piece of paper. After looking them over, select the top two strengths and the least damaging weakness and practice discussing them in preparation for this question. Be truthful; don't use canned answers. For example, "My weakness is that I'm a perfectionist," and "I'm a workaholic" are trite, overused, and may irritate your interviewer. But do figure out which of your weaknesses sounds least likely to cause a prospective employer concern and go with that one.

What do you know about our restaurant? or hotel, institution, or food service operation?

This is the opportunity to impress the hiring manager by showing that you had the initiative and drive to research the company before you came to the interview. Perhaps you saw the restaurant's executive chef at a recent culinary competition and were impressed by her work. Or you read an article praising the food improvements being made in the local hospital's food service department. Make sure you have something positive to say.

Why did you leave your last job?

No matter how bad the circumstances may have been, always frame your reason in a positive light. You might want to say something like "I wanted more responsibility" or "I wanted to advance my career." Don't ever say it was because you hated your boss.

How many days were you absent from work in your last job?

Of course you need to answer honestly, but be sure to phrase your answer in a positive light or offer an explanation for why you may have missed several days. If you didn't miss any days, don't just say "zero" or "none." Use the question as an opportunity to stress your high work ethic, sense of professionalism, or passion for excellence. For example, you might say, "I am proud to say that I did not miss one single day in my last position as line cook because I take my work very seriously, and I am committed to providing excellent service to the customers and to my employer."

While you need to answer questions in an interview clearly and concisely, you also need to ask questions. Asking the right questions can help you to determine if you really want to work for a particular organization.

Asking Questions

At some point during the interview, the interviewer will most likely ask you if you have any questions. If she doesn't, you'll need to bring it up yourself. You can simply say something like, "I also have a few questions for you to help me get a better sense of the position" and then plunge in. Have a list of questions ready to help you determine if the position is a good fit for you. Remember, it's not a one-way street—you are also evaluating them. Besides, if you don't ask any questions, you may give the impression that you are not interested in the position.

Here are some sample interview questions. You may have some other questions, but you can use this list as a starting point.

1. What would my typical day consist of?
2. What would my level of responsibility be?
3. What would my work hours be?
4. How many customers do you serve daily or weekly?
5. How long has this establishment been in business?
6. How often do you change your menu?
7. How many cooks work in this kitchen?
8. What is the possibility for promotion?
9. Do you team up trainees with experienced cooks? For how long?
10. What type of benefits do you offer?
11. What kind of incentives or bonuses are available?

Asking the right questions in an interview can give you the feedback you need to make a sound decision once your job offers start rolling in. While some interviews will inevitably go smoother than others, each one offers you a chance to practice and improve your interviewing skills. After each interview, remember to send a thank-you note to follow up on the meeting.

Follow Up After the Interview

After the interview, send a note to thank the interviewer for the opportunity to speak with her or him. Mention the time and date of the original interview, briefly highlight your qualifications, and reiterate your interest in the job. The interviewer may need to see other applicants before making an offer, so don't get discouraged if you don't get a definite answer right away. Generally, a decision is reached within a few weeks. If you do not hear from an employer within the amount of time suggested during the interview, follow up with a telephone call. However, don't call every day looking for an answer.

In addition to participating in actual job interviews, you can also get helpful job-related information by going on informational interviews.

Culinary Scoop

What is a patissier? A *patissier* is the French term for a pastry chef. Some people in the culinary arts use the terms interchangeably.

Informational Interviews

An informational interview is different from a job interview because you are merely seeking information and not an actual job. They are a good way to familiarize yourself with a new culinary position or area of specialization. For example, if you've only worked in restaurants, and you are interested in landing a job in a corporate dining room or hospital food service operation, you can contact someone who works in these areas and arrange an informational interview with them. Or if you've never set foot into a professional kitchen, but you're interested in exploring it, you can start by asking several cooks a few questions. You'll want to make maximum use of the time a person is willing to spend with you, so ask pertinent questions and be concise. Here is a list of questions that you can ask during an informational interview:

- What is your typical workday like?
- What things do you find most rewarding about your work?
- What are the toughest problems you encounter in your job?
- Please give me a general description of the work you do.
- What are the frustrations in your work?
- What educational degrees, professional certifications, or other credentials are needed for entry and advancement in this area?
- Do you belong to any professional associations? Do they provide job hunting assistance or post job openings?
- What abilities, interests, values, and personality characteristics are important for effectiveness and satisfaction in your field?
- How do people usually learn about job openings in your field?
- What types of employers, other than your own, hire people to perform the type of work you do?
- Do you know of any companies that offer entry-level training programs?
- If you were hiring someone for an entry-level position in your field, what would be the critical factors influencing your choice of one candidate over another?
- Is there anything else you think I would benefit from knowing about this field?

Conducting informational interviews will make you more knowledgeable about a particular job or area of specialization, and will also give you interview experience, which may lessen your anxiety in an actual job interview. Informational interviews are also an excellent opportunity for gaining networking contacts to help in your job search.

EVALUATING JOB OFFERS

So you've been offered a job, or better yet, several jobs. Your task now is to re-evaluate each job opportunity. How does each job stack up against the other? Perhaps one will give you the chance to work with a highly respected chef, perhaps another is right next door to your home, perhaps a third comes with an excellent benefits package. For many jobs, the places that offer you a position will not expect you to accept or reject an offer on the spot. You'll probably have a week or more to make up your mind. You need to consider all your options, review your notes from each interview, and then make a list of the pros and cons for accepting each job. The last step is to review your lists and choose the company with the most pros and the least cons. Then presto! You've landed yourself a great job, and now you can focus on how to succeed in your new job.

Auguste Escoffier (1847–1935)

Georges Auguste Escoffier has been called the greatest chef of the century and the father of modern cookery. Indeed, he revolutionized the art and practice of cooking and made French cuisine world famous. He also initiated the brigade system of organization in professional kitchens, where duties are divided among cooks who work as a team, each cook at a separate station, such as sauté, grill, and pantry.

Who:	Alex Darvishi, CEC, AAC (Certified Executive Chef, American Academy of Chefs)
What:	Executive Chef at Meridian Hills Country Club
Where:	Indianapolis, Indiana
How long:	Twenty-two years in the culinary arts field

Insider's Advice

It is a good idea to call a few places and ask if you can observe their kitchen before you decide to enter the culinary arts field. Doing so will help you face the reality of the long hours and hard work needed in this career. In addition, visit a few culinary schools and speak to some of the students about their program.

If you decide a culinary career is right for you, a good path to take is to become an apprentice for three years to get the real world experience that you need, and then enroll in a culinary school. During an apprenticeship, you get hands-on experience by going through all the different stations in the kitchen. With this firm foundation in place, you'll be able to absorb and understand more while in culinary school. After completing a culinary program, it takes many years of hard work and diligence to become a chef. Don't expect to graduate from high school, go directly into a two-year culinary training program, and come out as a chef.

The first thing to learn about cooking is the importance of the basics. Don't be one of those people who skip through the basics in a hurry to get to the more fancy aspects of cooking. For example, you should know how to properly braise meat for a basic pot roast—many cooks, and even some chefs, do not know how to do this basic task. First get a firm grasp of the basics, then you can branch out and do more advanced work.

Insider's Take on the Future

Because of the current shortage of trained staff, now is an excellent time to get into the field. You'll find many opportunities available all over the nation. Keep in mind that people are getting more education nowadays than in years past. Start by working for a well-educated top quality minded chef at a top quality establishment (do not expect top wages). Swallow your pride and learn all you can; do not expect these well-established chefs to come to you and teach you things. You need to observe, take notes, and take initiative. You need to dedicate yourself to the profession by putting in long hours at work and by continuing to educate yourself during your off-hours.

There is so much to learn about cooking that you must consider yourself a student for your whole career. Read books and magazines, browse the Internet, ask questions at work, get continuing education, and experiment on your own to continually expand your knowledge. After graduating from culinary school, continue working at a variety of top-notch establishments that are in different parts of the country and even abroad. After a few years, you will be ready to become a true chef.

CHAPTER | 6

You'll find out how to interact with supervisors, locate mentors, and achieve culinary certifications in this chapter. With these tips, hard work, and a little luck, you can advance to the level of executive chef or even own your own restaurant. You'll also find out about several related careers, such as food writer and educator. Profiles of successful chefs are included.

HOW TO SUCCEED ONCE YOU'VE LANDED THE JOB

You can achieve success in your culinary arts career in many ways. After you break into the field and gain experience, a variety opportunities will become available, ranging from attaining professional certifications to owning your own restaurant. You can also explore related career paths, from food stylist to dietitian to food technologist and more. Armed with the correct tools, you can attain any kind of professional success in the world of culinary arts.

STEPPING STONES TO SUCCESS

After you invest your time, energy, and financial resources to complete a training program and land a great job, it's time to find out as much information as possible about how you can succeed in that job and in your career as a whole.

Succeeding in a Professional Kitchen

When you start a new job as a culinary arts professional, you will most likely get some type of on-the-job training. In large restaurant kitchens, national franchise restaurants, or large hotels, the training will probably be more extensive and organized than in a small professional kitchen. Whatever the form of training available to you is, be sure to listen carefully, ask questions, and take notes after each shift to remember the important points.

Starting Out Success Tips

- Watch the head chef closely and listen carefully to directions.
- Volunteer to come in early or to work late for special occasions.
- Get to know your coworkers and supervisors.
- Work hard and move fast.
- Ask lots of questions.
- Read culinary books and magazines to expand your knowledge.
- Eat at other restaurants periodically to evaluate your competition.
- Actively plan and manage your career.

Chef Geraldine Born, a culinary educator, offers this advice to graduates of culinary schools who are working on the hotline in a professional kitchen: "Stay in a job for at least a year, and learn all you can from the chef. Then, if you need to move on, look for another good chef to work with." Indeed, during the early stages of your culinary career, focus on learning as much as you can from as many people as you can. Be prepared for difficult working conditions and long hours. Chef Timothy Rodgers, a department head at the Culinary Institute of America, has this to say about the beginning stages of a culinary career:

> You have to be able to put up with a lot of stuff at the beginning of
> your career. Chefs have the reputation of being egomaniacs. And I
> think the reason they got that way is because they had the ability to

put aside their ego to work for an egomaniac. The chefs they learned from probably taught them to become egomaniacs.

In the best places, you'll work the hardest and longest hours. You can always work less in the future. It's something to look forward to. If you start out working long hours, then it's easier to work fewer hours later in your career. This industry has many mediocre jobs and few great ones. If you want to work 40 hours in the formative stages of your career, then you're going to end up in positions where there isn't a lot of potential, challenge, or fulfillment. If you're willing to put in the time early on, then later on you can get the few jobs available in which you'll have a decent schedule.

FITTING INTO THE WORKPLACE CULTURE

As you progress in your career, you'll find that every professional kitchen is different—each one has its own flavor. You'll get a feel for the atmosphere in your kitchen after the first day or two. Stay alert and keep your eyes open to find out how things are run and the level of formality that is the norm. If you find that you're having trouble fitting into the kitchen environment, don't worry. It's not necessarily a sign that you need to switch jobs; it often takes time to adjust to new surroundings. Just focus on learning all you can and excelling in the tasks that you are given.

A Word About Women Cooks/Chefs

Women who become cooks or chefs may need to work a bit harder at fitting into the workplace culture. Strangely enough, the cooking profession is still dominated by men, although more and more women are entering the field all the time. Here are a few comments from women chefs in the field. Chef Sharon Odmann describes her experiences this way:

> I learned firsthand that women still are not accepted in this industry, even in this country. A male chef supervisor told me one day, "You're never going to amount to anything." Meanwhile, the male chef he hired was a crack addict, and I was doing all the work. I encountered discriminatory behavior at four more restaurants, so it wasn't something that was limited to one place. I found that the people were very hard; there was a lot of screaming, cursing, drugs, and sexual intim-

idation. By this time I was 45 years old, and I just didn't want to deal with all of that, so I started my own business. Currently, I am chef owner of the Kiyote Cowboy Cookery & Personal Chef Services.

Another chef speaks out on the realities many women face in this industry, and what you can do about it. Chef Mary Cannataro is planning to open her own restaurant in Maui. She says:

> In the different professional kitchens I've worked in, I didn't come across many other women. In fact, I was usually the only one. It's still a male-dominated field. Often a male chef would pull me aside and tell me, "You have to be careful because you're the only female in the kitchen, and you know how these guys are." Women often have to tolerate a lot of sexual harassment in this business. I suggest that women look for restaurants where several women work in the kitchen or hold management positions. In Chicago, for example, a restaurant I opened with three women from culinary school called *Tomboy* is a totally woman-run place. Although it has only been open for a year and a half, it's taken off like wildfire. While the trend is that more women are entering the field, I don't think there are yet enough women in the bigger industry places like hotels.
>
> It's common in this male-dominated field for women to get relegated to the pastry area. A male chef will often hire a woman and then just shove her into the pastry section. I've done a lot of pastry work, and I have my pastry certification, but I prefer the cooking end.

For more information about women cooks and chefs, contact the Women Chefs and Restaurateurs, an organization that provides networking support and other benefits to women in the industry; Appendix A lists their contact information. Or look for the book by Chef Ann Cooper entitled *A Woman's Place is in the Kitchen*.

Interacting with Supervisors

There is a lot of leeway in how to "best" interact with your supervisors. Some kitchens have an informal atmosphere in which everyone jokes with each other and engages in socializing during downtime. Other kitchens are more formal, and you need to be circumspect when addressing the sous chef, chef, and executive chef. Until you know for sure what the atmosphere is, you might want to play it safe, and assume it's somewhat formal when addressing your supervisors.

However, be sure to keep lines of communication open between you and your manager. Chef Mary Cannataro shares this advice:

> When you go to work for new chefs, let them know your career plans. Whenever there is time, ask the chef to show you how to do new things—tell her or him that you want to learn as much as you can. I learned a lot by saying "please show me this" or "I want to learn how to do that." If you don't speak up and let your intentions be known, the chef will think you're just there to do your job and go home. Good chefs will not be threatened by hearing your goals; they'll know that you're interested in doing more and may consider you when special projects arise.

Learning from Mentors

You'll probably need to actively search for a mentor, unless someone informally decides to take you under his or her wing and show you the ropes. The qualities of a good mentor are based on a combination of teaching ability, level of expertise in a certain area, and personality compatibility. Chef Timothy Rodgers, a Team Leader for Curriculum and Instruction at the Culinary Institute of America explains:

> You normally get promotions through movement to new positions and word of mouth. In my career, I filled out most of my job applications the first day I started working because I got the job based on someone's recommendation. It's a kind of mentoring thing.
>
> In fact, finding a mentor is the way to go. Find the best mentor you can. Look for people with the best names, the best reputations, best kitchens, best restaurants, and best hotels. Then it's a matter of personalities. If you're willing to do anything for this person and you respect them, then you're in the right position. If you can't stand the person and don't feel right about putting yourself out for their convenience and their causes, then you're in the wrong place.

There are several ways to find a mentor. Many people study industry magazines to see who is at the top in their area of specialization. If you want to learn about nouvelle cuisine, then you need to do some research to find out who the best chefs in nouvelle cuisine are. Also, can you relocate to work under the very top chefs in the field, or do you need to find an excellent chef locally? Another method is to just go visit several establishments and ask to speak to the chef to find out more about his or her cooking style. Other ways to find a mentor include asking for advice from instructors at culinary schools, surfing the Internet, and networking through culinary associations. Spending time and effort to find a mentor is an investment in your future.

Joining Professional Organizations

There are several culinary-related professional associations, and if you didn't already join one or more as a student member, you may want to consider joining at this stage of your career. One of the benefits of joining a professional culinary association is networking with others in the field. The two largest associations are the American Culinary Federation and the National Restaurant Association. Appendix A lists many more organizations that offer significant benefits to culinary professionals.

One example is the American Institute of Wine and Food (AIWF). Heidi Cusick is the director of education and programs for this organization. She explains that their membership includes both consumers and professionals, so the AIWF provides a forum for valuable dialogue between these two groups. She also says: "In terms of how this organization applies to culinary careers, this is one of the networking organizations to which you could belong to meet people in the field. I've been a member since 1983—I'm also a food, wine, and travel writer."

The Institute sponsors an annual international conference; the theme for the 1998 conference in New York City was *Elements of Taste*. In addition to annual conferences, there are over 30 local chapters that sponsor educational seminars and other events throughout the year. You can obtain more information about this nonprofit educational association by contacting their national headquarters office, listed in Appendix A.

CULINARY ARTS CERTIFICATIONS

Getting certified as a culinary arts professional can lead to new job opportunities and advancement, and it shows your commitment to your work. The culinary arts industry has several different levels of certifications that you can achieve as you progress through your career. Chef Charles Ciufi, CCC, CCE, president of the Suncoast Cooks and Chefs Association says:

> I believe that certification is the way to go. To really build your career, find out what you need to do to become certified, then go after it. It's becoming increasingly important in today's business climate for cooks and chefs to become certified. In fact, some large hotel chains

are currently working to get everyone who is at the sous chef level and beyond certified.

Whether you want to become a cook, pastry chef, executive chef, or other type of culinary professional, standards of certification are varied and often rigorous. In most cases, you'll need to possess a certain amount of education and experience, and you may need to pass a culinary exam as part of the certification process. Most certification programs charge fees ranging from $35 to well over a hundred dollars, although at least one program charges over $3,000.

You will gain prestige in the industry, respect from your peers, and a rewarding sense of accomplishment when you obtain a certification credential. Many esteemed chefs proudly list their certification designation letters after their name. Now you can find out what all those letters mean that appear behind a chef's name in a printed brochure or food magazine. Here's an explanation of the most commonly held certifications by culinary professionals. To find out more about a particular certification, see Appendix A to get the address or phone number for the organization that offers it. Then contact that association to obtain detailed information and application forms.

American Culinary Federation Certification Programs

The American Culinary Federation offers nine different certification designations. Here are the various levels of achievement you can aspire to:

Certified Master Chef (CMC)
Certified Master Pastry Chef (CMPC)
Certified Executive Chef (CEC)
Certified Executive Pastry Chef (CEPC)
Certified Culinary Educator (CCE)
Certified Chef de Cuisine (CCC)
Certified Sous Chef (CSC)
Certified Working Pastry Chef (CWPC)
Certified Culinarian (CC)
Certified Pastry Culinarian (CPC)

To get a better idea of what each certification level entails, take a look at the following chart listing the precise definition for each job. These are specific job descriptions established by the American Culinary Federation for each level of certification that they offer their members.

MASTER CHEF/MASTER PASTRY CHEF

The *master chef* or *master pastry chef* is an individual who possesses the highest degree of professional knowledge and skill. These chefs teach and supervise their entire crew as well as provide leadership and serve as role models to the ACF apprentices. Certification at this level requires both a theoretical and a practical examination of knowledge and skills.

EXECUTIVE CHEF

The *executive chef* is a full-time chef who is the department head responsible for all culinary units in a restaurant, hotel, club, hospital, or other food service establishment. He or she might also be the owner of a food service operation. The person in this position must supervise a minimum of five full-time persons in the production of food.

EXECUTIVE PASTRY CHEF

The *executive pastry chef* is the department head, usually responsible to the executive chef of a food operation or to the management of his/her employing research or pastry specialty firm.

CULINARY EDUCATOR

The *culinary educator* is a chef who is working as an educator at an accredited institution in a culinary or food service management program.

CHEF DE CUISINE

The *chef de cuisine* is the supervisor in charge of food production in a food service operation. This could be a single unit of a multi-unit operation or a free-standing operation. He or she is in essence the chef of this operation with final decision-making power as it relates to culinary operations. The person in this position must supervise a minimum of three full-time people in the production of food.

WORKING PASTRY CHEF

The *working pastry chef* is defined as the chef responsible for a pastry section or a shift within a food service operation.

SOUS CHEF

A *sous chef* is a supervisor of a shift, station, or stations in a food service operation. A sous chef must supervise a minimum of two full-time people in the preparation of food. Other job titles that qualify for this designation include: sous chef, banquet chef, chef garde manger, first cook, A.M. sous chef, and P.M. sous chef.

CULINARIAN/PASTRY CULINARIAN (Formerly Cook/Pastry Cook)

A *culinarian* is defined as a person positioned in any one station in a food service operation, responsible for preparing and cooking sauces, cold foods, fish, soups and stocks, meats, vegetables, eggs, and other items.

A pastry culinarian is defined as a person positioned in any one station in a food service operation, responsible for preparing and baking pies, cookies, cakes, breads, rolls, or other baked goods and dessert items.

Source: American Culinary Federation

To become certified, you must complete a required number of education and experience points, which vary according to the certification level you want to achieve. You can earn points by successfully completing levels of education ranging anywhere from a high school to a doctoral degree, and by passing mandatory courses in sanitation, nutrition, and supervisory management. Other education points may be earned by passing certification exams, participating in culinary competitions, attending industry meetings, and taking approved continuing education courses. Your culinary work experience must be documented by your employer.

Certification Exams

You'll need to take a written exam and include your passing score along with your certification application documents. The written exams for most of the levels of certification are administered by a national testing agency. The written exams are based on the following general culinary texts and references.

The Art & Science of Culinary Preparation by Jerald Chesser, 1st Edition

The New Professional Chef by the Culinary Institute of America, 6th Edition

Professional Cooking by Wayne Gisslen, 5th Edition

On Cooking by Sarah Labensky and Alan M. Hause

Practical Baking by William Sultan, 5th Edition

Professional Baking by Wayne Gisslen, 5th Edition

The Professional Pastry Chef by Bo Friberg, 2nd Edition

Since each exam emphasizes different areas of study, contact the ACF certification office at 800-624-9458 to request a subject outline for your specific exam, or get one from their Web site at http://www.acfchefs.org. You can also ask people who have already taken the exams what areas were emphasized and what specific books they recommend you study.

American Academy of Chefs (AAC)

A career move that is related to certification, but isn't actually called "getting certified" is applying for membership in the prestigious American Academy of Chefs. All nominations must be made by a local chapter of the American Culinary Federation and membership requirements are stringent. For example, you must be certified as Master Chef, Master Pastry Chef, Executive Chef, Executive Pastry Chef, or

Culinary Educator and continue to renew certification as required by ACF to become eligible for nomination to the American Academy of Chefs. Once you gain membership, you may place the letters AAC after your name.

Educational Foundation of the National Restaurant Association Certification

The Educational Foundation of the National Restaurant Association offers the designation of Certified Foodservice Management Professional (FMP) to individuals who meet education and experience criteria and who pass an exam in food service management. The exam, which lasts three hours, consists of 200 multiple-choice questions on topics that a food service manager needs to know. The five major areas are:

1. human resources/diversity
2. marketing
3. operations
4. risk
5. unit revenue and cost control

You can take the exam at the annual National Restaurant Association Show in Chicago each May, or you can contact your state restaurant association to see if they offer the exam. To pass the test, you must receive a grade of 75%. The FMP certification lasts for a lifetime, so you do not need to renew it. You can purchase a review notebook from the National Restaurant Association to review material in the five management areas that appear on the exam.

Educational Institute of the American Hotel and Motel Association Certification

While the Educational Institute of the American Hotel and Motel Association offers several different certifications for professionals in the hospitality industry, those which apply to culinary professionals are listed below.

Certified Hospitality Educator (CHE)

There are approximately 697 people who currently hold the CHE certification, and 400–500 more people who are in the process of earning it. The CHE program offers a four-day workshop that leads to certification, and its program is designed for post-secondary and high school hospitality educators. On the fourth day of the workshop, educators are given two hours to complete a test with 100 multiple-choice questions based on the workshop's content. Additional education and experience requirements exist, so contact the AHMA for more details.

Certified Food and Beverage Executive (CFBE)

To qualify for the CFBE certification, you must be an executive-level food and beverage manager in a hotel administration, food and beverage director/general manager, or a restaurant facility executive chef. Certain education and experience requirements also apply. Contact the AHMA for more information.

International Food Service Executives Association (IFSEA) Certification

The International Food Service Executives Association offers two different certifications: the Certified Food Manager (CFM) and Certified Food Executive (CFE). CFE is the higher level of certification, requiring more education and work experience than CFM. The IFSEA certification program has existed for 33 years and uses a point system to determine the qualifying amount of education and experience needed for each level. For example, you can earn points by graduating from a training program, attending industry conferences, participating in culinary competitions, or getting new members to join IFSEA.

International Association of Culinary Professionals Certification

You can apply for the Certified Culinary Professional (CCP) program through the International Association of Culinary Professionals. Earning this designation shows your high level of professional and ethical standards in the culinary field. You'll need to pass a two and a half hour exam consisting of multiple choice, true/false, and essay questions.

Examination Topics

- Asian
- baking
- food chemistry
- food identification
- foods of North America
- French
- Italian
- nutrition
- sanitation

In addition to passing the culinary exam, you'll need to complete a personal data profile, which uses a point system to determine if you possess the qualifying amount of education and experience to earn the certification. In addition to education and work experience, you can earn points by attending annual culinary conferences, holding a leadership position in a culinary association, publishing a culinary book or article, public speaking, volunteering, and earning culinary awards. You must also pledge to adhere to a code of professional ethics.

American Institute of Baking Certification

You can become a certified baker by completing the certification requirements established by the American Institute of Baking (AIB). The first step is to complete a correspondence course about the science of baking. Then, take two seminars that are offered at the AIB headquarters in Manhattan, Kansas. Finally, there are three different options you can specialize in: bread, cake, or cookie, each of which requires more seminars. Many courses are offered twice annually and last from one to four weeks. You must complete the program within three years.

PASS CERTIFICATION EXAMS ON YOUR FIRST TRY

Since many of the culinary certifications available to you require that you pass a written exam, it makes sense to review general test-taking guidelines. See Appendix B under *Test Preparation* for a list of test preparation books. Here are a few things that can increase your chances of achieving a passing score on certification exams:

- Set priorities on what material to study. You can't possibly learn every detail about the job level you want to obtain, so focus on the most important aspects. If you don't, you can easily get bogged down in wading through information that is not going to be tested on the exam.
- Make a study schedule several weeks or months before the exam and stick to it. Allow sufficient time each day for studying a section of material and don't forget to preview and review the material you study. A good study method is to create flash cards and test yourself on key concepts and questions that may appear on the test.
- Try studying with a partner to boost your chances of getting a passing score. If you know someone who is taking the same exam, ask him or her to study with you. Ask each other questions and discuss the topics

thoroughly a few hours each week for a month or two before the exam. Or have a friend quiz you on culinary arts terms or procedures.

Before you decide to take a culinary certification exam, ask yourself if you know the answers to all of the following questions. If you don't, it's time to contact the sponsoring association to find out the answers.

Questions to Ask Before Taking Your Exam

1. How can I register for the exam?
2. How soon can I take the exam?
3. How much does the exam cost?
4. Where can I take the exam?
5. What identification do I need to bring to the exam?
6. What should I bring to the test? (i.e., calculator, pencils, scratch paper)
7. What is the passing score for this exam?
8. How long will it take to find out my score?

ADVANCEMENT OPPORTUNITIES

Advancement opportunities for cooks and chefs are better than for most other food and beverage preparation and service occupations, according to the Bureau of Labor Statistics. Many cooks and chefs acquire higher-paying positions and new cooking skills by moving from one job to another. In addition to strong culinary skills, advancement also depends on one's ability to supervise less-skilled workers and limit food costs by minimizing waste and accurately anticipating the amount of perishable supplies needed.

Some cooks and chefs gradually advance to executive chef positions or kitchen management positions, particularly in hotels, clubs, or upscale restaurants. Some choose to start their own businesses as restaurant owners or caterers, while others become instructors in culinary training programs in high schools, culinary institutes, community colleges, or other academic institutions.

Advancement opportunities for culinary arts professionals may depend on any one or more of the following factors:

+ reputation in your area of specialization
+ years of experience in the field
+ quantity and quality of professional contacts

- availability of management positions
- growth of the establishment
- level and type of education
- management and leadership skills

You may have all the qualifications, motivation, and skills needed to become an executive chef, but there may not be any openings available at your current establishment. You can either wait for an opening to occur, or you can apply for a job someplace else. Or if you want to branch out on your own, you could open your own restaurant or catering company.

You have to determine what is important to you when considering advancement opportunities, so that your career choices fit into an overall plan. For instance, you might find that it's time to change jobs when you no longer feel challenged in your current position. By getting another job in a different place, you can, in essence, give yourself a promotion. You may get any one or more of these benefits from a move:

- experience with different types of cuisine
- chance to work with a new chef
- higher pay or better health benefits
- better training programs
- higher-quality cooking or baking equipment
- learning how to deal with different types of coworkers
- chance to work in a restaurant with a better reputation
- better work schedule

The length of time you stay at any one job is a very personal decision. Some cooks and chefs stay in one place for many years, while others move to a new location every year or two. Take a long look at your current situation to see if you are still learning new things, are challenged with new opportunities, and are still feeling creative. If not, it may be time to move on to new challenges.

Advancing to Become a Chef

Don't be tempted to become a chef too soon. Once you become a chef, you may lose out on learning experiences that you could have had by working under other chefs. Spend a few years learning a variety of cooking methods and styles and developing your palate. Even if you go to a prestigious culinary school, don't feel like you should leave school and land a job as a chef right away. In fact, many chefs agree that would be a mistake. For example, Chef Mike Nipper in Palm Harbor, Florida says, "you don't graduate culinary school as a *chef*. You graduate with the *tools* to become a chef." Additionally, Chef Timothy Rodgers in Hyde Park, New York says, "resist the temptation to become a chef too soon. Once you're the chef, the learning opportunities become fewer and fewer."

After you spend a few years completing a formal culinary education and learning from successful chefs, you may be ready to become a chef yourself. Most chefs hold management positions—they are responsible for hiring, training, and overseeing the work of the kitchen staff. So once you become a chef, new challenges will arise. Here's some advice from Mary Cannataro, a chef in Chicago, Illinois:

> Be very tolerant of your waitstaff; don't get a big head and order people around. And never feel like you're too high up to dig in and do the work alongside your staff. It helps promote teamwork. You're always going to have chefs who feel that they know so much more than everyone else that they can act any way they please. However, I do see a trend of more caring people becoming chefs.

Executive Chef

After working as a chef for a few years, you may set your sights on becoming an executive chef. The responsibilities of executive chefs vary depending on the establishment in which they work. In a small restaurant, the executive chef may also be the sauté cook or saucier in addition to the kitchen manager, or the general manager of the entire establishment, or sometimes the owner. In a large restaurant or resort, the executive chef rarely does any cooking. Indeed, most executive chefs spend the majority of their time on administrative and management issues.

Therefore, becoming an executive chef is not for everyone. If you love the adrenaline rush of cooking 200–400 or more meals in a couple of hours every night, then you may want to advance your career by finding better paying jobs as a line cook, instead of becoming an executive chef. If you decide you would like to make the transition to executive chef, you may still be able to cook a limited number of items, such as the sauces or specials. The exact duties of executive chefs vary greatly depending on the size and type of the establishment in which they work. However, the typical job duties of an executive chef often include the following:

- managing the kitchen staff
- preparing work schedules

- deciding which ingredients to order
- negotiating supply costs with vendors
- placing orders for supplies
- evaluating the quality of products ordered
- computing costs
- decreasing food waste
- estimating food consumption
- creating or changing menus
- creating dinner specials
- overseeing food preparation and cooking
- examining the size of food portions
- hiring and firing staff
- finding ways to increase productivity
- managing the dishwashing staff
- checking the quality of food that leaves the kitchen

If you want to become an executive chef, you should have good health, stamina, self-discipline, initiative, leadership ability, problem-solving skills, and attention to detail. Executive chefs also need good communication skills to deal with customers and suppliers, as well as to motivate and direct their subordinates.

Many executive chefs have the initials CEC following their name to show that they have earned the designation of *Certified Executive Chef* from the American Culinary Federation (ACF). Chefs often need to have a significant amount of education and experience before they are granted the CEC designation.

OPENING YOUR OWN RESTAURANT

Many cooks and chefs want to open their own restaurants. Perhaps you also share this dream. If so, be careful, because without proper planning, this dream can quickly turn into a nightmare. Restaurants often have exorbitant start-up costs, so you'll need a lot of money just to get off the ground. In addition to the financial toll are the physical and emotional aspects of working extremely long hours for many months, or even years, while the restaurant struggles to turn a profit. On the other hand, owning a restaurant can bring you great rewards. You get to be your own boss and have the autonomy to express your creativity on your own terms. Chef Mary Cannataro, who is planning to open her own restaurant in Maui next year, has this advice:

First, work as hard as you can for as many places as you can. When you feel like you've learned enough or know as much as you can about a place, move on to another. Save lots of money. Have an *excellent* business plan—and have *lots* of confidence in yourself, or you'll never succeed. Also, understand that with your own place you need to be willing to work 18–20 hour days sometimes, and you need to have management skills, too. Both front and back of the house knowledge is necessary, as well as some knowledge of janitorial and appliance repair. You'll never be able to afford (at the beginning, anyway) to call someone to unplug a sink or fix something every time one little thing goes wrong.

If you would like to open your own restaurant some day, you can take some entrepreneurial courses at a local college or university to help you decide whether or not to go this route. Your small business instructors can help you weigh the pros and cons of your proposed venture. It can be a difficult decision to make because the failure rate of new restaurants is high. While no one knows exactly what the failure rate is, some sources claim that 80% of new restaurants fail within their first year. You can increase your chances of being one of the restaurants that succeed by conducting research, seeking expert advice, and creating a winning business plan.

Here are several things to consider before opening a restaurant:

- availability of funding
- location of restaurant
- atmosphere of dining room
- type of customer to be served
- type and price of food served
- availability of labor pool
- cost and types of licenses needed
- whether or not to serve liquor
- what the hours of operation will be

You can gain valuable information to help you make decisions on these key areas by conducting research. For example, look at the demographics of the locations you are considering. How dense is the population in a five-mile radius? What are typical income levels of people in the surrounding area? Find out as much as possible about your prospective customers to help you decide which type and price of cuisine to offer. Resources are available from the U.S. Census of Population that list demographic profiles, income levels, and types of housing in particular neighborhoods. You can purchase these lists from the U.S. Bureau of the Census—check your phone book for a branch office near you.

In addition, you can take a survey of the people in the neighborhood to see what type of restaurant they would like to frequent. Talk to other business owners in the area to get an idea of the level of traffic and to find out if business is seasonal or strong year-round. Contact a few real estate agents who specialize in commercial sales and ask them questions about each site you're considering. Also, learn about the local zoning codes, ordinances, and licenses that are required. You can find out more about these regulations by contacting the local chamber of commerce or city zoning office. Another resource is the Small Business Administration (SBA). This organization provides free assistance with writing business plans, loan and financing guidelines, and free consulting through SCORE, the Service Corps of Retired Executives. Check your phone book for a chapter near you.

After you've completed significant research and assembled all the ingredients for success, you get to look forward to your grand opening. It could either be a hectic and busy few hours or an extremely slow eternity. This is where strong marketing and publicity skills come in to play. You need to find ways to draw people into your new restaurant. Consider the advertising budget carefully, and don't be afraid to spend money on this key aspect of the business. If your opening night goes well, you'll get to breathe a large sigh of relief before moving on. During the first few weeks of business, you'll want to keep a close eye on food supplies. Are you running out of key ingredients on a regular basis, or are you throwing out spoiled food because you ordered too much of one thing? These are key areas in which you can curb costs and improve your bottom line.

Culinary Scoop

What is a restaurateur? A *restaurateur* is a person who owns or operates a restaurant.

Franchise Restaurants

Many restaurateurs are flocking into the franchise restaurant business because it's experiencing such significant growth. While it is a challenge to break in, it can be done. If you would like to get into the restaurant franchise business some day, you might want to do some investigating of this option. The first step to opening a franchise is to approach several different franchise parent companies to find out what their terms and policies are. Once you sign an agreement with one, you'll get a license to the name, trademark, and concept of the restaurant. In return, you pay the franchise parent company several fees and/or royalties. You'll need to conform to the guidelines of operation that the parent company establishes. In fact, random inspections are normally conducted anonymously by the parent company to ensure you are meeting their standards of operation. You normally receive the following benefits from a franchise parent company:

- licensed use of trademark, inventory management system, special equipment, and secret recipes
- exclusive territorial rights to the franchise
- significant training programs including manuals, booklets, and videos
- advertising benefits
- discounts from main suppliers to the restaurant chain
- management assistance and continuing education for staff
- a leased building for the site of the restaurant

If opening your own restaurant seems to be too large a step to take, you can open a catering company.

STARTING A CATERING COMPANY

Launching your own catering company is a good way to go into business for yourself without the exorbitant costs of opening a restaurant. You can monitor how much business you take in and schedule vacation time for yourself by simply not taking on business during those times. You may find that you get extremely busy during the summer months catering outdoor parties and events and then again in the fall and winter months around Thanksgiving and Christmas, so you can plan vacations for early spring. A great deal of satisfaction can come from this flexibility in your schedule and being your own boss.

Some caterers prepare food in their own kitchens and then transport it, while other caterers prefer to cook everything at the events. Be sure to find out the health restrictions and certifications that are needed in your state for each of these catering methods.

Before you decide to jump into the unknown waters of owning a catering company, it's a good idea to get specific experience in the field. Sharon Odmann, chef owner of a catering company, gives this advice:

If you want to start your own catering business, work for a caterer first. That way you don't have to reinvent the wheel. Caterers have experience you can learn from; they know what their clients want. Even if you only work for a caterer for six months to a year, you'll gain a lot. This is sometimes called *retained earnings*—you are learning a lot but you aren't getting paid very much. However, later in your career, you'll profit from having gained that experience.

While caterers need to be extremely organized and have strong culinary skills, they also should understand the psychology of serving people. Learning the nuances of how to provide excellent service to guests while containing costs can help you immeasurably. Chef Odmann describes two examples of this:

One thing you can learn from a caterer is how to set up a buffet table. You need to understand the psychology of what the guests see when they step up to a buffet table. If the table is flat and just has platters of food on it, the guests may be disappointed even before they taste any of the food. However, if the table is artfully arranged, multileveled, and pleasing to the eye, guests feel they will be getting something special. There are other valuable tips you can learn from caterers too, such as cost control. For example, if you place the inexpensive items at the beginning of the line, such as bread, salad, and potatoes, then the guest already has a full plate and is happy about how much food there is before she even gets to the prime rib or roast beef at the end of the line and may not take as much of the more expensive items.

After you gain experience working for a caterer and decide to open your own catering business, remember that several niche markets exist. Research each market before you decide which one to focus on. Perhaps you want to cater banquets in reception halls, or small parties for individual clients, or big corporate meals served on a daily basis. There are several opportunities available in the catering field, so don't limit yourself. After you build up your business and are realizing significant profits, you may want to open a catering hall and offer your services on your own premises. Once you break into this field, you have many options available to advance your career and succeed as a chef caterer.

RELATED CAREER OPTIONS

The culinary arts field offers numerous career choices, whatever your basic interests and abilities may be. Certain related career options could involve going to college or even graduate school for in-depth study of subjects such as management, food science, or journalism. To find out more about the wealth of opportunities available in related careers, take a look at the following job descriptions.

Food Writer/Editor

There are many areas of specialization within the realm of a food writer or editor. Perhaps you want to write cookbooks. Well, there is certainly a growing market for them—according to the American Booksellers Association, Americans bought some 38 million cookbooks in 1996. Or perhaps you want to be a restaurant critic, a journalist, a book reviewer, or a food historian. You might recognize some of these food writers who have left their stamp on the world of culinary arts: Craig Claiborne, James Beard, M.F.K. Fisher, and Elizabeth David.

Perhaps you'd like to become a food editor for a magazine, newspaper, or Internet site. Food Editor Kim O'Donnel found her position after graduating from Peter Kump's New York Cooking School. Here's how she broke into the field:

> I have a background in journalism, covering hard news. I also did freelance writing in Johannesburg, South Africa. When I returned to the States, I taught English as a Second Language for a while but gradually began spending more time working in a bakery, eventually becoming the manager. Then, to prepare myself for cooking school, I took two jobs—one was to plate desserts on the weekend at a busy restaurant in Washington, D.C. Then I did what I call an "apprenticeship" for a well-known chef. I called and called and called this chef until she let me come in and be her slave. I worked for her full-time for four months before I headed off to cooking school.
>
> After graduating from Peter Kump's New York Cooking School, I moved back to Washington and began interviewing for cooking jobs. A friend mentioned that someone was looking for a freelance food writer, but as it turns out, he was looking to fill a full-time position. I walked in casually but ended up being interviewed for my current position. I was hired to launch the food section of an arts and entertainment guide on the Internet for Washingtonpost.com. The food

and restaurant section has been very active because we focus on cooking, and we devote our energy to creating multi-media original and exclusive content that is found only on the Internet. I'm closely connected to food, I'm writing, and I'm teaching people how to do things they might not have otherwise known.

Food Stylist

Food stylists prepare food for photo shoots for magazines, newspapers, and books. They also market foods and food products on television. Food stylists are often responsible for creating the entire setting in which the food—the subject of the photograph—appears. Many cook or bake the food to be photographed, while others work in conjunction with a baker or chef. Food stylists arrange food to make it look appealing. They also may set up the backdrop for the photo session by arranging other items to appear near the food, such as a vase of flowers, a bowl of fresh fruit, holiday trimmings, or other items that fit into a theme. For example, for a photo of three enchiladas, the background items may include a colorful blanket, a sombrero, or a piñata. The food stylist often works closely with the photographer to decide upon the placement of items on the set.

Food Photographer

Food photographers may specialize in photographing just food, or they may photograph food along with other subjects. They work with food stylists to set the stage for a photo shoot by arranging the light source and placing the camera at appropriate angles. Formal training or experience in photography along with a knowledge of the culinary arts will help you succeed in this field. Food looks different through the eye of the camera than it does to the naked eye. For example, any blemish on a tomato, as soon as it is photographed, will stand out and become the focal point of the picture. Food photographers also need to be aware of the intended audience and know what the desired outcome of the photography session is. Therefore, they must possess strong communication skills to interact with and understand food stylists, magazine producers, authors, book editors, and chefs. They also must exercise patience in this exacting field since one photo could take an entire day to complete.

Cook or Chef in Research and Development Kitchens

Cooks and chefs can also work in research and development kitchens for magazines and food manufacturers. They create and test recipes that will appear in a magazine or cookbook. Cooks who create recipes may work for themselves, a magazine or book publisher, or another organization. Some work on a freelance basis, getting a flat fee for each recipe they create or test. Others become authors of cookbooks and test their recipes as a part of writing the book. Cooks and chefs who work for food magazines are often food writers; they cook special dishes and then write about them for the magazine. They may conduct research to find new and unusual ingredients or to find new ways to use traditional ingredients. A particular type of cuisine may be featured in one issue of a magazine, so the chefs will have to research and develop all the different foods to be included in that issue. Food manufacturers employ cooks and chefs to develop recipes for new products and to research ways to alter existing products. For instance, a manufacturer may want to find a way to cut out half the fat from a particular item. Cooks or chefs would then research and test ways to create a good-tasting product in a new, low-fat way.

Food Technologist/Scientist

Food technologists or scientists conduct research to find new and improved ways to preserve, package, and deliver foods. They use scientific principles to examine food and determine how much protein, fat, and sugar is in each type of food. Some food technologists spend their time researching new food sources, while others search for substitutes to harmful additives or preservatives in food, such as nitrites. In addition to this research, some food technologists spend time in test kitchens testing new products. They may also work in laboratories to develop or refine methods for processing different types of food. Most food technologists work in the food processing industry, research universities, or the federal government. A bachelor of science degree is normally needed to land a job as a food technologist, and advanced degrees are also common.

Culinary Arts Instructor

Culinary arts professionals who are interested in teaching have a wealth of options available to them. Since the culinary arts field is growing and more schools are opening, the demand for chef instructors is rising. They are needed at public and private high schools, community and technical colleges, universities, and culinary institutes. Instructors may provide training for people with no experience or for cooks who are seeking continuing education courses. Experienced chef instructors may organize new programs, revise portions of the curriculum, and manage other instructors in addition to their teaching duties. Many chef instructors are responsible for teaching students in a production kitchen that cooks food for an on-campus restaurant, cafeteria, or bake shop.

Dietitian

Dietitians provide information about what proper nutrition is and how it can be obtained through food selection. Therefore, they are sometimes called nutritionists. They promote healthy eating habits in schools, hospitals, prisons, and corporations, as well as in large restaurant chains. They plan nutrition programs and individual meals that meet the national guidelines for nutritional requirements to help prevent and treat illnesses.

Some dietitians specialize in catering to the nutritional needs of hospital or nursing home patients with specific dietary requirements. They scientifically evaluate clients' diets and suggest modifications, such as less salt for those with high blood pressure or reduced fat and sugar intake for those who are overweight.

According to the Bureau of Labor Statistics, employment of dietitians is expected to grow about as fast as the average for all occupations through the year 2006. Dietitians and nutritionists held about 58,000 jobs in 1996. To become a dietitian, you need a bachelor's degree with a major in dietetics, foods and nutrition, food service systems management, or a related area.

Culinary Scoop

What is mirepoix? *Mirepoix* is a mixture of cut-up vegetables, usually consisting of carrots, celery, and onions, that is used to flavor stocks, soups, stews, and other foods.

SNAPSHOTS OF SUCCESS

You may be wondering how others entered the field of culinary arts and built successful careers for themselves. Well, here are some career snapshots to give you an idea of how some of today's chefs got their start in the culinary world.

Chef Department Head at Culinary Institute

Here's a look at how Chef Timothy Rodgers started his career in the culinary arts and moved on to achieve success as Team Leader for Curriculum and Instruction, Meat, and Garde Manger at the highly esteemed Culinary Institute of America in Hyde Park, New York. He explains:

> I started my culinary career in an old-model apprenticeship, which offered meals, housing, and a paycheck. I wanted to leave home, and someone came and said "I've got a great opportunity for you," so I went. It was the first time I was ever in a professional kitchen. I was introduced to the chef, who was an old-style European type chef—and he was king. Everyone looked up to him, and he had a lot of authority and responsibility. It was very regimented and disciplined in his kitchen. That was my first exposure to the culinary arts; I had never cooked anything in my life. I loved the discipline and the whole concept of taking pride in your work and enjoying your work.
>
> After finishing my apprenticeship, people whom I respected advised me to get a cooking diploma. I didn't want to go to school at first, but I became convinced and decided to go to the best school around—the Culinary Institute of America. I graduated with an A. O. S. degree.
>
> I'm currently a department head for the Meat and Garde Manger department at the Institute. I have about 14 chefs in my department. Each chef is responsible for his or her own facilities and students. I've had a lot of areas of specialization in my career in addition to meat and garde manger, including nutrition, Italian, and French. I came to the Institute for a year or two as an education sabbatical from the industry, and ended up staying for 10 and a half years. There are a lot of opportunities here—I've had the opportunity to do a PBS television cooking series, work on other video productions, and participate in the production of book projects.

Chef Owner of Catering Company & Personal Chef Services

Now meet another chef who had quite a different experience. Chef Sharon Odmann owns Kiyote Cowboy Cookery & Personal Chef Services. She relates how she entered the culinary arts field:

I made a career change into the culinary arts, although I was in a related industry. I held a fast-track corporate position for six years in a company that makes a product that is added to puréed foods for people in nursing homes with dysphasia. We started an industry of eye-appealing pureed foods, and I traveled across the country showing doctors, nurses, and dietitians our product. I was a single mom, and I had a nanny because I was away from home so much of the time. One day I asked my daughter to do something and she looked at the nanny and said, "Do I have to?" and that's when I realized this was all wrong; it was backwards. So I left that job to take some time off. I decided to work as a waitress because it seemed relaxing after the previous six years. One day I walked into the kitchen while the food service manager was preparing stuffed chicken breasts for a banquet. I was very interested in what he was doing and he was tired of it, so he said I could take over the banquets if I wanted. Within three weeks, I became the banquet chef. I then went to Harrisburg Community College, where I graduated with an associate degree in Culinary Arts.

Currently, I am chef owner of the Kiyote Cowboy Cookery & Personal Chef Services. What I like most about my business is that I'm serving people. Being a servant is a really powerful position—it's almost biblical. You're giving people what they really need. Even though we live in a service world, not many people are providing the service that people want. I love it when we do a party and it turns out better than the hostess expected it to. It's very fulfilling to me.

Chef of Clubhouse in Private Resort

A third snapshot shows how Chef Michael Nipper started his career in the food and beverage industry. He recounts:

I began my career as a busboy in a prestigious restaurant in Des Moines, Iowa, when I was 16 years old. I had the good fortune of working for a very talented, people-oriented manager. I worked my way up through front-of-the-house positions—working in the bar, then becoming a bartender, a waiter, and finally the floor manager. After six years, my manager left to open his own Italian restaurant, and I went with him—we were voted the best restaurant in Des Moines for several years. The chef who was hired for this new restaurant had gone to culinary school, and when I saw the great things he was doing, I was amazed.

I had never been exposed to that caliber of food and its preparation, presentation, and flavor. So I began volunteering my personal time to work in the kitchen for this new chef during the day. I was only able to work under the new chef's instruction for about a month because my work responsibilities expanded. However, about three months later, the chef asked me to work for him as a line cook. Thankfully, my manager supported my career change, so I went to work in the kitchen. I worked all the stations and then became the sauté cook—a very fast-paced position. In French, sauté literally means *to jump*.

Chef Nipper graduated from the New England Culinary Institute and is now a chef at the Island Clubhouse at the Westin Innisbrook Resort in Florida. He manages a staff of 10 cooks and other kitchen workers. He shares this about his current position:

I often take on the role of expediter myself, so I can be the conduit between the front and the back of the house staff. I assure the quality of each plate's presentation before it leaves the kitchen. We have two or three daily dinner specials in the restaurant—they are a great way to showcase our cooking. I like to encourage my staff to experiment and plan their own specials, so they also feel a sense of ownership. We don't change our regular menu too often because we have an established clientele who enjoy coming back for their favorite dishes. All in all, I have worked really hard to get where I am, and I'm proud to be a chef here at Innisbrook.

As you can see from these snapshots, there are many ways to enter the field, advance your career, and achieve success in the exciting field of culinary arts. If you pursue each step of your culinary arts career with diligence, perseverance, and commitment to excellence, you also will be able to achieve great success in your career.

A Cook's Tools

Three of the most important tools that cooks need in a professional kitchen are:

- a sharp knife
- a pair of tongs
- a dry towel

Who:	Kim O'Donnel
What:	Producer of *Food and Restaurants* for Washingtonpost.com (also known as a Food Editor)
Where:	Washington, D.C.
How long:	Four years in the culinary arts field

Insider's Advice

To become a food editor or writer, you really need to be a journalist, and you'll be a better food journalist if you have a cooking school background. I would never recommend that someone coming right out of a cooking school try to become a food writer or editor. They are still separate fields: journalism and cooking. You need to have some type of experience in both fields to make it work. So if you don't have a background in writing, you'll be hitting a dead-end even if you have years of cooking experience.

If you want to break into the field of food writing, try to get experience as a freelancer, volunteer, or intern at a weekly or community newspaper. Submit proposals on a freelance basis for restaurant reviews or profiles of chefs. Since the public has developed an interest in cooking and chefs, this type of story will probably be picked up by food editors. Work on building a portfolio of published pieces.

In addition, going to cooking school is a really valuable thing. It's a concentrated chunk of time—you're eating, sleeping, and breathing cooking—you're in school 40 hours a week. You don't have time to think about anything else, so I definitely recommend that type of experience to people interested in food writing.

Insider's Take on the Future

I think that the world of food and cooking on the Internet is really going to grow, and that is where the opportunities are going to be in the future. The atmosphere is more informal on the Internet, so some food writers even pitch article ideas via e-mail messages.

A lot of food journalists have been in the business for a very long time and there is a need for younger voices in a lot of the food magazines and cookbooks.

The upcoming generation of food journalists will have a more solid background in cooking. For example, more food journalists in their 20s and 30s are taking the route of going to cooking school, and their mentors are encouraging them to do so.

APPENDIX A

This appendix contains a list of local and national professional associations and accrediting agencies. You can contact them to obtain information related to employment or training as a culinary arts professional. Also included are higher education departments in each state—you can contact them for information on state financial aid programs.

PROFESSIONAL ASSOCIATIONS

Contact any of the following professional organizations to find out more information about the culinary arts field. Internet addresses and fax numbers are included where available.

American Association of Family and Consumer Sciences
1555 King St.
Alexandria, VA 22314-2752
703-706-4600
FAX: 703-706-4662
http://www.aafcs.org

American Correctional Food Service Association
4248 Park Glen
Minneapolis, MN 55413
612-928-4658; 612-929-1318

American Culinary Federation
10 San Bartola Dr.
P. O. Box 3466
St. Augustine, FL 32085-3466
904-824-4468; 800-624-9458
FAX: 904-825-4758
http://www.acfchefs.org

American Dietetic Association
216 W. Jackson Blvd., Ste. 800
Chicago, IL 60606-6995
312-899-0040
FAX: 312-899-1979
http://www.eatright.org

American Hotel and Motel Association
1201 New York Ave., NW, Ste. 600
Washington, DC 20005-3931
202-289-3100
FAX: 202-289-3199
http://www.ahma.com

American Institute of Baking
1213 Bakers Way
Manhattan, KS 66502
785-537-4750; 800-633-5137
FAX: 785-537-1493
http://www.aibonline.org

The American Institute of Wine & Food
1550 Bryant St., Ste. 700
San Francisco, CA 94103
415-255-3000; 800-274-AIWF
FAX: 415-255-2874

American Personal Chef Institute
4572 Delaware St.
San Diego, CA 92116
800-644-8389

American Society for Hospital Food Service Administrators
American Hospital Association
840 North Lake Shore Dr.
Chicago, IL 60611
312-280-0000

The Bread Bakers Guild of America
P. O. Box 22254
Pittsburgh, PA 15222
412-322-8275
FAX: 412-322-3412
http://www.bbga.org

Career College Association
750 First St. NE, Ste. 900
Washington, DC 20002-4242
202-336-6700
FAX: 202-336-6828

Careers Through Culinary Arts Program, Inc.
155 West 68th St.
New York, NY 10023
212-873-2434
FAX: 212-873-1514

Chefs de Cuisine Association of America
155 E. 55th St., Ste. 302B
New York, NY 10022
212-832-4939

Club Managers Association of America
1733 King St.
Alexandria, VA 22314
703-739-9500

Confrérie de la Chaîne des Rôtisseurs
444 Park Ave. South, Ste. 301
New York, NY 10016-7321
212-683-3770
FAX: 212-683-3882
http://www.chaineus.org/

The Cooking Advancement Research and Education Foundation (CAREF)
304 West Liberty St., Ste. 201
Louisville, VA 22314
502-587-7953

Council on Hotel, Restaurant, and Institutional Education
National Restaurant Association
1200 17th St. NW
Washington, DC 20036-3097
202-331-5990
FAX: 202-785-2511
http://www.chrie.org

Dietary Managers Association
406 Surrey Woods Dr.
St. Charles, IL 60174
630-587-6336; 800-323-1908
FAX: 630-587-6308

Educational Foundation of the National Restaurant Association
250 South Wacker Dr., #1400
Chicago, IL 60606-5834
312-715-1010; 800-765-2122
FAX: 312-715-0807
http://www.edfound.org

Educational Institute of the American Hotel and Motel Association
P. O. Box 1240
East Lansing, MI 48826-1240
800-349-0299
FAX: 517-372-5141
http://www.ei-ahma.org

Foodservice Consultants Society International
304 W. Liberty St., Ste. 201
Louisville, KY 40202-3068
502-583-3783
FAX: 502-589-3602
fcsi@fcsi.org

Hospitality Business Alliance
Educational Foundation of the National Restaurant Association
250 South Wacker Dr., #1400
Chicago, IL 60606-5834
312-715-1010; 800-765-2122
FAX: 312-715-0807
http://www.edfound.org

Hotel Employees and Restaurant Employees International Union
1219 28th St. NW
Washington, DC 20007
202-393-4373

Independent Bakers Association
1223 Potomac St., NW
Washington, DC 20007
202-333-8190
FAX: 202-337-3809

Institute of Food Technologists
221 N. LaSalle St., #300
Chicago, IL 60601-1291
312-782-8424
FAX: 312-782-8347
http://www.ift.org

International Association of Culinary Professionals
304 West Liberty St., Ste. 201
Louisville, KY 40202
502-581-9786; 800-928-4227
FAX: 502-589-3602
http://www.iacp-online.org

International Food Service Executive's Association
1100 South State Rd. 7, Ste. 103
Margate, FL 33068
954-977-0767; 954-977-0874
http://www.ifsea.org

The James Beard Foundation, Inc.
167 W. 12th St.
New York, NY 10011
212-675-4984; 800-36-BEARD
FAX: 212-645-1438

Les Dames d'Escoffier
P. O. Box 2103
Reston, VA 20195-0982
703-716-5913
FAX: 703-758-4902
http://www.ldei.org

National Association of Catering Executives
60 Revere Dr., Ste. 500
Northbrook, IL 60062
847-480-9080
FAX: 847-480-9282

National Association of Colleges and Universities Food Services
1405 S. Harrison Rd.
Manly Miles Bldg., Ste. 305
Michigan State University
East Lansing, MI 48824-5242
517-332-2494
http://www.nacufs.org

National Association for the Specialty Food Trade, Inc.
120 Wall St., 27th fl.
New York, NY 10005-4001
212-482-6440
FAX: 212-482-6459

National Restaurant Association
1200 17th St., NW
Washington, DC 20036-3097
202-331-5900; 800-424-5156
FAX: 202-331-2429
http://www.restaurant.org

Retailer's Bakery Association
14239 Park Center Dr.
Laurel, MD 20707
301-725-2149; 800-638-0924
FAX: 301-725-2187

Roundtable for Women in Foodservice
1372 La Colina Dr. #B
Tustin, CA 92780
714-838-2749; 800-898-2849
FAX: 714-838-2750
http://www.rwf.org

Service Employees International Union
1313 L St. NW
Washington, DC 20005
202-898-3200
FAX: 202-898-3402

Share Our Strength
1511 K St. NW, Ste. 940
Washington, DC 20005
202-393-2925; 800-969-4767

Society of Wine Educators
8600 Foundry St.
Mill Box 2044
Savage, MD 20763
301-776-8569
FAX: 301-776-8578
http://www.wine.gurus.com

United Food and Commercial Workers International Union
1775 K St. NW
Washington, DC 20006
202-223-3111
FAX: 202-466-1562

U. S. Pastry Alliance
3349 Somerset Trace
Marietta, GA 30067
770-980-0071; 888-APASTRY
FAX: 770-980-9573
http://www.uspastry.org

United States Personal Chef Association
4769 Corrales Rd.
Corrales, NM 87048
800-995-2138
FAX: 505-899-4097
http://www.uspca.com

Vatel Club (social club for chefs)
244 Madison Ave., #362
New York, NY 10016-2817
212-246-9397

Waiters Association
12162 SW Schoolls Ferry Rd., #80
Tigerd, OR 97223
503-524-0788
FAX: 503-524-4183

Women Chefs and Restaurateurs
110 Sutter St., Ste. 210
San Francisco, CA 94104
415-362-7336
FAX: 415-362-7335
http://www.chefnet.com/wcrc/wcr.html

NATIONAL ACCREDITING AGENCIES

Here is a list of national agencies for you to contact to see if your chosen school is accredited. You can request a list of schools that each agency accredits.

Accrediting Commission of Career Schools and Colleges of Technology
2101 Wilson Blvd., Ste. 302
Arlington, VA 22201
703-247-4212
FAX: 703-247-4533

Accrediting Council for Continuing Education and Training
1560 Wilson Blvd., Ste. 900
Arlington, VA 22209
703-525-3000
FAX: 703-525-3339

Accrediting Council for Independent Colleges and Schools
750 First St. NE, Ste. 980
Washington, DC 20002-4241
202-336-6780
FAX: 202-842-2593

American Culinary Federation Education Institute Accrediting Commission
10 San Bartola Dr.
P. O. Box 3466
St. Augustine, FL 32085-3466
800-624-9458
FAX: 904-825-4758

American Dietetic Association
Commission on Accreditation
216 W. Jackson Blvd., Ste. 800
Chicago, IL 60606-6995
312-899-0040; 800-877-1600
FAX: 312-899-1979

Council of Hotel, Restaurant, and Institutional Education
1200 17th St. NW
Washington, DC 20036-3097
202-331-5990
FAX: 202-785-2511

REGIONAL ACCREDITING AGENCIES

If your school is not accredited by one of the national agencies, it may be accredited by a regional one. Here is a list of regional agencies that you can contact to see if your chosen school is accredited. They are organized by broad geographic regions.

Middle States

Middle States Association of Colleges and Schools
Commission on Institutions of Higher Education
3624 Market St.
Philadelphia, PA 19104-2680
215-662-5606
FAX: 215-662-5950

New England States

New England Association of Schools and Colleges
Commission on Institutions of Higher Education
209 Burlington Rd.
Bedford, MA 07130-1433
617-271-0022
FAX: 617-271-0950

New England Association of Schools and Colleges
Commission on Vocational, Technical and Career Institution
209 Burlington Rd.
Bedford, MA 01730-1433
617-271-0022
FAX: 617-271-0950

North Central States

North Central Association of Colleges and Schools
Commission on Institutions of Higher Education
30 North LaSalle, Ste. 2400
Chicago, IL 60602-2504
312-263-0456
FAX: 312-263-7462

Northwest States

Northwest Association of Schools and Colleges
Commission on Colleges
11130 NE 33rd Place, Ste. 120
Bellevue, WA 98004
206-827-2005
FAX: 206-827-3395

Southern States
Southern Association of Colleges and Schools
Commission on Colleges
1866 Southern Lane
Decatur, GA 30033-4097
404-679-4500; 800-248-7701
FAX: 404-679-4558

Western States
Western Association of Schools and Colleges
Accrediting Commission for Community and Junior Colleges
3402 Mendocino Ave.
Santa Rosa, CA 95403-2244
707-569-9177
FAX: 707-569-9179

Western Association of Schools and Colleges
Accrediting Commission for Senior Colleges and Universities
c/o Mills College, Box 9990
Oakland, CA 94613-0990
510-632-5000
FAX: 510-632-8361

STATE HIGHER EDUCATION OR FINANCIAL ASSISTANCE AGENCIES

You can request information about financial aid from each of the following state higher education agencies and governing boards. Internet addresses have been included when available.

Alabama Commission on Higher Education
100 North Union St.
Montgomery, AL 36104
334-242-2539

Alaska Commission on Postsecondary Education
3030 Vintage Boulevard
Juneau, AK 99801-7109
907-465-2962
http://sygov.swadm.alaska.edu/BOR/

Arizona Commission for Postsecondary Education
2020 North Central Ave., Ste. 275
Phoenix, AZ 85004-4503
602-229-2591
http://www.abor.asu.edu/

Arkansas Department of Higher Education
114 East Capitol St.
Little Rock, Arkansas 72201-3818
501-371-2000

California Student Aid Commission
P. O. Box 510845
Sacramento, CA 94245-0845
916-445-0880
http://www.ucop.edu/ucophome/system/regents.html

Colorado Commission on Higher Education
1300 Broadway, 2nd Floor
Denver, CO 80203
303-866-2723
http://www.state.co.us/edu_dir/state_hredu_dept.html

Connecticut Department of Higher Education
61 Woodland St.
Hartford, CT 06105-2391
800-566-2618
http://www.lib.uconn.edu/ConnState/HigherEd/dhe.htm

Delaware Higher Education Commission
Carvel State Office Bldg., 4th fl.
820 North French St.
Wilmington, DE 19801
302-577-3240
http://www.state.de.us/high-ed/commiss/webpage.htm

District of Columbia Department of Human Services
Office of Postsecondary Education, Research and Assistance
2100 Martin Luther King, Jr., Ave., SE, Ste. 401
Washington, DC 20020
202-727-3688

Florida Department of Education
Office of Student Financial Assistance
255 Collins Bldg.
Tallahassee, FL 32399-0400
904-487-0049
http://www.nwrdc.fsu.edu/bor/

Georgia Student Finance Commission
State Loans and Grants Division
2082 East Exchange Place, Ste. 200
Tucker, GA 30084
770-414-3000
http://www.peachnet.edu/BORWEB/

Hawaii State Postsecondary Education Commission
2444 Dole St., Room 209
Honolulu, HI 96822-2394
808-956-8213
http://www.hern.hawaii.edu/hern/

Idaho State Department of Education
650 West State St.
Boise, ID 83720
208-334-2270
http://www.sde.state.id.us/

Illinois Student Assistance Commission
1755 Lake Cook Rd.
Deerfield, IL 60015-5209
847-948-8500

State Student Assistance Commission of Indiana
150 West Market St., Ste. 500
Indianapolis, IN 46204-2811
317-232-2350
http://www.ai.org/ssaci/

Iowa College Student Aid Commission
200 Tenth St., 4th fl.
Des Moines, IA 50309-2824
800-383-4222
http://www.state.ia.us/government/icsac/index.htm

Kansas Board of Regents
700 S. W. Harrison, Ste. 1410
Topeka, KS 66603-3760
913-296-3517

Kentucky Higher Education Assistance Authority
1050 U. S. 127 South, Ste. 102
Frankfort, KY 40601-4323
800-928-8926

Louisiana Student Financial Assistance Commission
Office of Student Financial Assistance
P. O. Box 91202
Baton Rouge, LA 70821-9202
800-259-5626

Finance Authority of Maine
119 State House Station
One Weston Court
Augusta, ME 04333-0949
207-626-8200
http://www.maine.edu

Maryland Higher Education Commission
16 Francis St., Jeffrey Bldg.
Annapolis, MD 21401-1781
410-974-2971
http://www.ubalt.edu/www/mhec/

Massachusetts Board of Higher Education
330 Stuart St., Ste. 304
Boston, MA 02116
617-727-9420

Michigan Higher Education Assistance Authority
Office of Scholarships and Grants
P. O. Box 30462
Lansing, MI 48909-7962
517-373-3394

Minnesota Higher Education Services Office
Capitol Square Bldg., Ste. 400
550 Cedar St.
St. Paul, MN 55101-2292
800-657-3866
gopher://gopher.hecb.state.mn.us/

Mississippi Postsecondary Education
Financial Assistance Board
3825 Ridgewood Rd.
Jackson, MS 39211-6453
601-982-6663

Missouri Coordinating Board for Higher Education
3515 Amazonas Dr.
Jefferson City, MO 65109-5717
800-473-6857
gopher://dp.mocbhe.gov/

Montana University System
2500 Broadway
Helena, MT 59620-3103
800-537-7508
http://www.montana.edu/~aircj/manual/bor/

Nebraska Coordinating Commission for Postsecondary Education
P. O. Box 95005
Lincoln, NE 68509-5005
402-471-2847

Nevada Department of Education
Capitol Complex
700 E. Fifth St.
Carson City, NV 89710
702-687-9227
http://nsn.scs.unr.edu/nvdoe/

New Hampshire Postsecondary Education Commission
2 Industrial Park Dr.
Concord, NH 03301-8512
603-271-2555

State of New Jersey
Office of Student Financial Assistance
4 Quakerbridge Plaza, CN 540
Trenton, NJ 08625
800-792-8670
http://ww.state.nj.us/highereducation/

New Mexico Commission on Higher Education
1068 Cerrillos Rd.
Santa Fe, NM 87501-4925
800-279-9777
http://www.nmche.org/index.html

New York State Higher Education Services Corporation
99 Washington Ave.
Albany, NY 12255
518-474-5642
http://hesc.state.ny.us

North Carolina State Education Assistance Authority
P. O. Box 2688
Chapel Hill, NC 27515-2688
919-549-8614

North Dakota University Systems
600 East Boulevard Ave.
Bismarck, ND 58505-0230
701-328-4114

Ohio Student Aid Commission
309 South Fourth St.
Columbus, OH 43215
888-833-1133
http://www.bor.ohio.gov

Oklahoma State Regents for Higher Education
500 Education Bldg.
State Capital Complex
Oklahoma City, OK 73105
800-858-1840
http://www.ogslp.org

Oregon State System of Higher Education
700 Pringle Pkwy., S. E.
Salem, OR 97310-0290
503-378-5585
http://www.osshe.edu/

Pennsylvania Higher Education Assistance Agency
1200 North Seventh St.
Harrisburg, PA 17102-1444
717-720-2800
http://sshe2.sshechan.edu/sshe.html

Rhode Island Higher Education Assistance Authority
560 Jefferson Boulevard
Warwick, RI 02886
800-922-9855

South Carolina Higher Education Tuition Grants Commission
P. O. Box 12159
Columbia, SC 29211
803-734-1200
http://che400.state.sc.us

South Dakota Department of Education and Cultural Affairs
Office of the Secretary
700 Governors Dr.
Pierre, SD 57501-2291
605-773-3134
http://www.state.sd.us/state/executive/deca/deca.html

Tennessee Student Assistance Commission
404 James Robertson Pkwy., Ste. 1950
Nashville, Tennessee 37243-0820
800-342-1663
http://www.TBR.state.tn.us

Texas Higher Education Coordinating Board
P. O. Box 12788, Capitol Station
Austin, Texas 78711
800-242-3062
http://www.texas.gov/agency/781.html

Utah State Board of Regents
Utah System of Higher Education
355 West North Temple
#3 Triad Center, Ste. 550
Salt Lake City, UT 84180-1205
801-321-7100
http://www.gv.ex.state.ut.us/highered.htm

Vermont Student Assistance Corporation
Champlain Mill
P. O. Box 2000
Winooski, VT 05404-2601
800-642-3177
http://www.vsac.org

Virginia Council of Higher Education
James Monroe Bldg.
101 North Fourteenth St.
Richmond, VA 23219
804-225-2623
http://www.schev.edu

Washington Higher Education Coordinating Board
P. O. Box 43430
917 Lakeridge Way, SW
Olympia, WA 98504-3430
360-753-7850

West Virginia Higher Education Grant Program
1018 Kanawa Boulevard East, Ste. 700
Charleston, WV 25301-2827
304-558-4614
http://www.scusco.wvnet.edu/

Wisconsin Higher Education Aids Board
P. O. Box 7885
Madison, WI 53707-7885
608-267-2206
http://www.uwsa.edu/

Wyoming Student Financial Aid
University Station, Box 3335
Laramie, WY 82071
307-777-7763

U.S. Department of Education
Office of Postsecondary Education
Student Financial Assistance Programs
Pell and State Grant Section
ROB #3, Room 3045
600 Independence Ave., SW
Washington, DC 20202-5447
202-708-4607

Division of Higher Education Incentive Programs
Higher Education Programs
Office of Postsecondary Education
U. S. Department of Education
1280 Maryland Ave., SW, Ste. C80
Washington, DC 20024

APPENDIX B

For more information on the topics discussed in this book, refer to the following book list organized by subject. The list of books is followed by a list of culinary arts periodicals.

ADDITIONAL RESOURCES

BAKING

Amendola, Joseph, and Donald Lundberg. *Understanding Baking, 2nd Edition.* John Wiley & Sons, 1992.

Friberg, Bo. *The Professional Pastry Chef, 3rd Edition.* John Wiley & Sons, 1996.

Sultan, William J. *Practical Baking, 5th Edition.* John Wiley & Sons, 1990.

COVER LETTERS

Beatty, Richard H. *The Perfect Cover Letter. 2nd Edition.* John Wiley & Sons, 1997.

Fein, Richard. *Cover Letters, Cover Letters, Cover Letters, 2nd Edition.* Career Press, 1998.

Toropov, Brandon. *Last Minute Cover Letters.* Career Press, 1998.

Wood, John. *How to Write Attention-Grabbing Query & Cover Letters.* Writers Digest Books, 1996.

Yate, Martin. *Cover Letters That Knock 'Em Dead, 3rd Edition.* Adams Media Corporation, 1998.

CULINARY ARTS

Cooper, Ann. *A Woman's Place is in the Kitchen.* John Wiley & Sons, 1997.

Cullen, Noel C. *The World of Culinary Supervision, Training, and Management.* Prentice-Hall, 1995.

Donovan, Mary Deirdre (Editor), and the Culinary Institute of America. *The New Professional Chef (TM).* John Wiley & Sons, 1996.

Dornenburg, Andrew, and Karen Page. *Becoming a Chef: With Recipes and Reflections from America's Leading Chefs.* John Wiley & Sons, 1995.

Eberts, Marjorie, Margaret Gisler, and Linda Brothers. *Opportunities in Fast Food Careers* (VGM Opportunities Series). VGM Career Horizons, 1995.

Escoffier, Auguste. *The Escoffier: A Complete Guide to Modern Cooking.* Crown Publishing, 1971.

Gisslen, Wayne. *Professional Cooking, 4th Edition.* John Wiley & Sons, 1999.

Kamman, Madeleine. *The New Making of a Cook: The Art, Techniques, and Science of Good Cooking.* William Morrow and Company, 1997.

Labensky, Sarah R. *Applied Math for Food Service.* Prentice-Hall, 1997.

Labensky, Sarah R., and Alan M. Hause. *On Cooking: Techniques from Expert Chefs, 2nd Edition.* Prentice-Hall, 1999.

Labensky, Steven, Sarah Labensky, and Gaye Ingram. *Webster's New World Dictionary of Culinary Arts.* Prentice-Hall, 1997.

Lang, Jennifer Harvey (Editor). *Larousse Gastronomique: The New American Edition of the World's Greatest Culinary Encyclopedia.* Crown Publishers, 1988.

Larousse, David Paul. *The Professional Garde Manger: A Guide to the Art of the Buffet.* John Wiley & Sons, 1996.

McGee, Harold. *On Food and Cooking: The Science and Lore of the Kitchen.* Simon & Schuster, 1984.

Ruhlman, Michael. *The Making of a Chef: Mastering Heat at the Culinary Institute of America.* Henry Holt and Company, 1997.

Zagat Survey 1998 America's Top Restaurants (Serial). Zagat Survey, LLC. 1998.

FINANCIAL AID

College School Service. *College Costs & Financial Aid Handbook, 18th Edition.* The College Entrance Examination Board, 1998.

Davis, Kristen. *Financing College: How To Use Savings, Financial Aid, Scholarships, and Loans to Afford the School of Your Choice.* Random House, 1996.

Schwartz, John. *College Scholarships and Financial Aid. 7th Edition.* Arco Publishing, 1997.

FOOD STYLING AND PHOTOGRAPHY

Carafoli, John, and Rosalind Smith. *Food Photography and Styling: How to Prepare, Light, and Photograph Delectable Food and Drinks.* Amphoto, 1992.

Hichs, Roger, and Frances Schultz. *Food Shots (Pro-Lighting).* Rotovision, 1995.

FOOD WRITING

Holm, Kirsten (Editor). *1999 Writer's Market (Annual).* Writers Digest Books, 1998.

Linford, Jenny. *Writing About Food.* A&C Black, 1996.

INTERVIEWS

Bloch, Deborah P. *Have A Winning Job Interview.* VGM Career Horizons, 1997.

Krannich, Caryl Rae, and Ronald L. Krannich. *101 Dynamite Answers to Interview Questions: Sell Your Strengths, 3rd Edition.* Impact Publications, 1997.

Morgan, Dana. *The 10 Minute Guide to Job Interviews.* Macmillan General Reference, 1998.

Yeager, Neil, and Lee Hough. *Power Interviews.* John Wiley & Sons, 1998.

JOB HUNTING

Adams Media Staff. *Adams Jobs Almanac 1998.* Adams Media Corporation, 1997.

Bolles, Richard Nelson. *What Color is your Parachute? A Practical Manual for Job Hunters and Career Changers.* Ten Speed Press, 1999.

Cubbage, Sue A. and Marcia P. Williams. *The 1997 National Job Hotline Directory.* McGraw-Hill, 1997.

Sonnenblick, Carol, Michaele Basciano, and Kim Crabbe. *Job Hunting Made Easy: 20 Simple Steps to Coming Up a Winner.* LearningExpress, 1997.

NETWORKING

Alexander, Laurel. *Career Networking: How to Develop the Right Contacts to Help You Throughout Your Working Life.* Trans-Atlantic Publications, 1997.

Kramer, Marc. *Power Networking: Using the Contacts You Don't Even Know You Have to Succeed in the Job You Want.* VGM Career Horizons, 1998.

Shelly, Susan. *Networking for Novices: The Basics Made Easy.* LearningExpress, 1998.

RESTAURANT OWNERSHIP

Association of Small Business Development Centers, Woody McCutchen, and Ann Dugan, eds. *Franchising 101: The Complete Guide to Evaluating, Buying and Growing Your Franchised Business.* Upstart Publishing Company, 1998.

Bradach, Jeffrey L. *Franchise Organizations.* Harvard Business School Press, 1998.

Marvin, Bill. *Guest-Based Marketing: How to Increase Restaurant Sales Without Breaking Your Budget.* John Wiley & Sons, 1997.

Rainsford, Peter and David H. Bangs. *The Restaurant Start-Up Guide.* Upstart Publishing Company, 1997.

RESUMES

Adams Resume Almanac & Disc. Adams Media Corporation, 1996.

Grappo, Gary Joseph, and Adele Lewis. *How to Write Better Resumes, 5th Edition.* Barron's Educational Series, 1998.

Potter, Ray. *100 Best Resumes for the 21st Century.* Macmillan General Reference, 1998.

Reed, Jean. *Resumes That Get Jobs, 9th Edition.* Arco Publishing, 1998.

STUDY SKILLS IMPROVEMENT

Coman, Marcia J., and Kathy L. Heavers. *How to Improve Your Study Skills, 2nd Edition.* NTC Publishing Group, 1998.

How to Study: The Basics Made Easy in 20 Minutes a Day. LearningExpress, 1997.

Practical Math Success in 20 Minutes a Day. LearningExpress, 1997.

Read Better, Remember More: The Basics Made Easy in 20 Minutes a Day. LearningExpress, 1997.

TEST PREPARATION

ACT: Powerful Strategies to Help You Score Higher: 1998 Edition. Simon & Schuster: Kaplan, 1997.

Katyman, John, and Adam Robinson. *Cracking the SAT, 1998 Edition.* Random House: The Princeton Review, 1998.

Secrets of Taking Any Test: The Basics Made Easy in 20 Minutes a Day. LearningExpress, 1997.

WORK RELATIONSHIPS

Bell, Arthur H., and Dayle M. Smith. *Winning With Difficult People, 2nd Edition.* Barron's Educational Series, 1997.

Bramson, Robert M. *Coping With Difficult Bosses.* Simon & Schuster, 1994.

Felder, Leonard. *Does Someone at Work Treat You Badly?* Berkley Books, 1993.

Weinstein, Bob. *I Hate My Boss! How to Survive and Get Ahead When Your Boss is a Tyrant, Control Freak, or Just Plain Nuts!* McGraw-Hill, 1998.

CULINARY ARTS PERIODICALS

Here are some magazines and journals that might interest you.

Art Culinaire
40 Mills Street
Morristown, NJ 07960
201-993-5500

Bon Appetit
5900 Wilshire Blvd.
Los Angeles, CA 90036
213-965-3600
http://www.epicurious.com

Chef
20 North Wacker, Ste. 3230
Chicago, IL 60606
312-849-2220

Chile Pepper: The Magazine of Spicy Food
1227 W. Magnolia Ave.
Ft. Worth, TX 76104
888-SPICYHOT
http://www.chilepeppermag.com

Chocalatier
45 West 34th St.
New York, NY 10001
212-239-0855

The Cookbook Review
60 Kinnaird St.
Cambridge, MA 02139
617-868-8857

Cooking Light
2011 Lake Shore Dr.
Birmingham, AL 35209
205-877-6000
http://www.pathfinder.com/cl

Cook's Illustrated
17 Station St., Box 1200
Brookline, MA 02147
617-232-1000

Culinary Review
1246 North State Pkwy.
Chicago, IL 60610-2219

Culinary Trends
6285 East Spring St.
Long Beach, CA 90808
714-826-9188

Eating Well
Ferry Rd.
Charlotte, VT 05445
802-425-3961

Food & Wine
1120 Avenue of the Americas, 10th fl.
New York, NY 10036-6700
212-382-5600
http://www.pathfinder.com/foodwine

Food Arts
387 Park Ave. South
New York, NY 10016
212-684-4224

Gourmet
560 Lexington Ave.
New York, NY 10022
212-880-8800
http://www.epicurious.com

Nation's Restaurant News
425 Park Ave.
New York, NY 10022
212-756-5000
http://www.nrn.com

Pastry Art & Design
45 West 34th St.
New York, NY 10001
212-239-0855

Restaurant Business
633 Park Ave. South, 3rd fl.
New York, NY 10010-1789
212-592-6200

Restaurant Hospitality
1100 Superior Ave.
Cleveland, OH 44114
216-696-7000

Restaurants and Institutions
1350 E. Touhy Ave.
Des Plaines, IL 60018
708-635-8800

Saveur
100 Avenue of the Americas
New York, NY 10013
800-462-0209
212-334-2400

Vegetarian Times
4 High Ridge Park
Stamford, CT 06905
203-321-1758

Wine Spectator
387 Park Ave. South
New York, NY 10016
212-684-4224